Campaigns Of Curiosity; Journalistic Adventures Of An American Girl In London

Banks, Elizabeth L., 1870-1938

Campaigns

OF

Curiosity

Journalistic Adventures of an American Girl in London

"NO FRINGE ALLOWED."

BY

Elizabeth L. Banks

F. Tennyson Neely

Publisher

Chicago   New York

Neely's Library of Choice Literature { No. 38, Dec. 1894. Issued monthly. $6.00 a year. Entered at Chicago Post Office as Second-Class Matter.

CAMPAIGNS OF CURIOSITY

ELIZABETH L. BANKS.

(From a Photograph by the London Stereoscopic Company.)

CAMPAIGNS OF CURIOSITY

JOURNALISTIC ADVENTURES OF AN
AMERICAN GIRL IN LONDON

BY

ELIZABETH L. BANKS

F. TENNYSON NEELY,

CHICAGO.   Publisher: NEW YORK.

1894.

CONTENTS.

———◦◇◦———

LIST OF ILLUSTRATIONS.

PREFACE.

WHEN, a little over a year ago, I arrived in London with a star-spangled banner in my pocket, I had no intention of remaining long enough to make any extensive experiments in the line of the "newer journalism." I had only "taken a run" over to England to visit Westminster Abbey, St. Paul's, and the Tower, expecting then to return home and write up my "impressions" of London and Londoners.

"Don't forget that you are an American, and are going to England simply to compare the inferiorities of that country with the superiorities of your own." This was the parting injunction of a certain American editor when I left New York.

For some time after my arrival I not only never forgot that I was an American, but I took particular pains that nobody else should forget it. I waved the Stars and Stripes on every possible occasion, and sighed for an opportunity to defend my country. It was not long in coming, for I had been in London but a little over two weeks when Mr. Rudyard Kipling's criticisms of America appeared in the *Times*. My patriotic outburst, which I headed " An American Girl's Reply to Mr. Kipling," was printed in the same paper a few days later, and Uncle Sam sent me his congratulations across the water. That was the beginning of my journalistic career in London—a career that has not been without its pleasures as well as some very hard work.

At the end of a few months I began to like
London so well that I decided to stop longer, in
order to study something more than the "inferiorities" that my patriotic American co-worker had
bidden me seek, so I hung up my flag in the hall
where it might be seen without being too obtrusive,
and turned my attention to active work.

When I wrote my "In Cap and Apron" experiences for the *Weekly Sun*, I determined to say
nothing about my nationality, and in correcting the
proofs I thought I divested the narrative of all obvious
Americanisms.   But, alas! it was the "wash-bowls"
and "pitchers" that betrayed me.

"Does not Miss Banks know how to use proper
English, that she says 'bowl' instead of basin, and
'pitcher' instead of jug?" wrote an irate matron to
one of the papers, and the Editor of the *Weekly Sun*
was severely criticised for allowing "vulgar American" to appear in its columns.   Another lady
declared that I must be a person of strangely car-
nivorous tastes to demand a meat breakfast, which
led to a letter from someone else, who gave it as her
opinion that I must have come from America, a land
where the inhabitants breakfasted off chops and
steaks and buckwheat cakes.   Many epistles came to
me personally: some from ladies who seemed to be
under the impression that I had come to London to
set up the servants against the mistresses, and I was
requested to return to America before I raised an
insurrection.

On the other hand, the servants looked upon
me as a sort of Moses II., come to deliver them
out of the hand of their oppressors, and the con-

gratulatory letters that some of them sent me were rather amusing. After I finished my description of my life at Mrs. Allison's, and began to write concerning my experiences at Mrs. Brownlow's—I need hardly say that I have not given the real names or addresses of these people in any case—everybody turned round about face. The mistresses concluded that I was not half bad, after all; while the servants abused me because I advised them that it was wrong "to break and not tell." One housemaid, in her rage, wrote that she had intended suggesting that I be made an officer of the Domestic Servants' Protective League, but now I would be denied that honour, as every "proper servant" in London was my enemy.

During the time that I was relating my experiences as housemaid and parlourmaid, Mrs. Allison and Mrs. Brownlow received condolences from many quarters, though it appeared to me that the sympathy was wasted; for neither of them were such objects for public pity as some people seemed to imagine. Mrs. Allison, in particular, was looked upon as a deeply-injured woman, a sort of martyr, "butchered," as one writer expressed it, "to make a journalistic holiday." So far as I have been able to discover, no serious consequences attended my house-maiding exploit at Mrs. Allison's. To be sure, the scrubbing was woefully neglected during my *régime,* but otherwise the housemaid's duties were not so badly performed.

To those who understand how small the world really is, it will not appear strange that Mrs. Allison and I should have mutual acquaintances. Quite recently a friend invited me to accompany her to a

Sunday " at home," where, I was assured, I would be welcomed by a charming hostess and meet most agreeable people. The house to which she would have taken me was that of Mrs. Allison, of Portman Square! On hearing the name, I suddenly remembered that I was " writing against time," and the printers were waiting for copy. I have several times met my former mistress and her daughters on the street, and at the theatre we have often been near neighbours; but my change of costume proved a good disguise, and I doubt if they would know me unless I appeared to them in the garb of cap and apron.

The Brownlows forgave me for the deception I had practised upon them, and then went to America, to recuperate their fortunes, which, Mr. Brownlow said, had suffered considerably through the mistakes of the Cleveland Administration.

The criticism which my " In Cap and Apron " articles excited was mild when compared with that called out by the appearance in the *St. James's Gazette* of " The Almighty Dollar in London Society " series. Not even yet am I able to understand how I merited it. I have felt somewhat in the position of the unlucky cat which suffered drowning at the hands of the cruel Johnnie Green, although, according to the nursery rhyme—

"It never did him any harm,
But caught the mice in his father's barn."

When I acted the part of an American heiress, I not only exposed the methods by which certain English aristocrats sold their social influence, but I held up to ridicule the shoddiness of some of my own country-people, who are well known on two sides of the

Atlantic. In explaining that Lady —— chaperoned Miss Porkolis for a particular sum of money, I did not attempt to excuse the young Chicagoan for her part in the transaction ; for, surely, the purchaser of social distinction is not a whit better than the person who turns it into a marketable commodity. Furthermore, I have not put forward Lady —— as being a typical specimen of all those who move in high society, any more than I have portrayed the representative American girl in Miss Porkolis. My object was but to show that the confidence Americans are accused of having in the purchasing power of "the almighty dollar" has not been altogether misplaced. I have noticed that the Colonial papers, especially those of Australia, have looked upon my American heiress campaign in the light of a huge joke played upon the aristocracy. A New Zealand Editor, in commenting upon the letters I received in answer to my advertisement for a chaperon, sighs for a peep into my desk, which, he thinks, must be brimful of interesting material that has not yet appeared in print. So far as those letters are concerned, I could safely hand him over the key ; for, aside from what is now in print, nothing of that interesting correspondence remains with me. Those who requested the return of their letters received them, and the rest were long ago consigned to the flames.

As regards the chapter in which I describe my search for a pedigree, it is but another instance of what dollars and sovereigns will do. I do not, however, hold up these would-be aristocrats as typical Americans. In the great hustle and bustle of our American life, dead and gone ancestors play no part.

So thoroughly do we believe in ourselves that self-confidence might almost be said to amount to self-sufficiency. We demand of a man not who his father was, but what he is himself. Yet, among over sixty millions of people, there must necessarily be a few snobs by way of variety, and that their money allows them to come to London to purchase the social precedence that is denied them at home, and a line of ancestors made to order, is a misfortune to America and England alike.

To the Editor of the *English Illustrated Magazine* I am indebted for the privilege of republishing the two articles which recount my experiences as a flower-girl and a crossing-sweeper. They do not take up any very serious social or moral problems, and so need not be further referred to here.

My trial at laundry work was the most difficult task I have yet attempted, and that I lived through it, and long enough to put the adventure into print, is a fact that still causes me to wonder. The relation of my experiences, coming at a time when the question of shorter hours and more perfect sanitation for laundries has been brought before Parliament by the Home Secretary, I hope may not be without the effect of calling attention to a class of working girls who stand in great need of a helping hand from the better classes.

If my exploits have done nothing more than to give many of my journalistic co-workers topics for some exceedingly clever and humorous "copy," they have not been altogether wasted. From the land of prose into the realm of poesy, Mr. Walter Besant wandered to tell the readers of the *Queen* something concerning the ambitions of "The Lady Housemaid." Mr. George R. Sims has given to the manufacturers of American furniture a valuable advertisement by describing for his "Referereaders" the wonderful transformations that took place in the star-spangled drawing-room where he called to interview me concerning the remarkable feats I performed as a parlourmaid, besides finding a plot for one of his ever-entertaining "dramas of the day." "The Coming of Elizabeth" has been graphically portrayed in the columns of *Judy* by a writer who, despite my effort to "calculate, reckon, and guess" as to his identity, is yet unknown to me by name. *Punch*, in a page devoted to the doings of "The Irrepressible She," has hinted to its readers what they have soon to dread, if the progressive "lady journalist" is allowed to pursue the uneven tenor of her way. The *Daily News*, in a witty review of my "In Cap and Apron" series, complimented me on my journalistic prowess, but deplored my inability to sew on a button and my general lack of feminine accomplishments. "Autolycus," in the *Pall Mall Gazette*, gallantly defended me from the attack of an enemy in the *Weekly Sun*, who, in proclaiming the opinion that I had never been in service at all, gave me credit for such imaginative faculties as would bring me a fortune and spare me much labour, time, and expense. In the *Lady's Pictorial*, "Mary Jane" covered herself with ink and glory by her smart sketches in which she depicted her ambitious attempt to leave off housework and "learn all about jernalism in two days." I prophesy for "Mary Jane" a brilliant future as a combined critic and sketch artist.

Numerous other weekly and daily journals have instructed and entertained their readers at my expense. The Press of my native land has also smiled approvingly upon me, and sent me invitations to return to the scenes of my early journalistic endeavours.

I have been impressed by the kindly feeling that the women journalists of London have shown towards me and the interest they have exhibited in my work. Especially is this true of the members of the Pioneer and Writers' Clubs. Coming here a stranger from over the sea, I was warned in the beginning by a cynical "gentleman journalist" that I would be looked upon as an interloper; but this has been far from the case, and among my co-workers in London I count many friends.

From the Editors of the various London papers, also, I have received the most courteous consideration and friendly advice, although, to be sure, some of them have smilingly referred to my adventures as "escapades" which they have appeared to consider a sort of journalistic sowing of wild oats.

Finally I wish to make my acknowledgments to the advertising columns of the daily papers. They have rendered me valuable assistance, without which these "CAMPAIGNS OF CURIOSITY" could never have been written.

E. L. B.

CAMPAIGNS OF CURIOSITY.

IN CAP AND APRON.

CHAPTER I.

"LIBERTY" AND "INDEPENDENCE."

"STITCH! stitch! stitch!" I stood in the doorway of a fifth-floor back-room in a Camberwell lodging-house, listening to a modern edition of "The Song of the Shirt," sung to the accompaniment of the sewing-machine. The scenery was similar to that painted by Thomas Hood half a

B

century ago. The woman and the unwomanly rags, the crust of bread, the table, the straw, and the broken chair, all were there. The singer of the song sat at the machine, her head bent over the work which her hands were guiding, while her feet pushed the treadle up and down. I looked on until my brain grew weary with the monotony of her movements and the grating noise of the unlubricated wheel.

"How much do you earn a day at that work?" I asked.

"Eighteenpence, Miss," was the answer.

"And you pay for your lodging, food and clothes, all with that eighteenpence?"

"Yes, Miss."

"But is there no other work you can do—nothing that is less wearing on body and brain?"

"Nothing, Miss. Some other girls that write a good hand get work in the City at £1 a week, and some that are quick at figures earn almost as much in the shops; but I can only sew. I bought my machine on time, and it's not paid for yet. Excuse me, but I must be on with my work."

Stitch! stitch! stitch! The noise commenced again.

"Stop!" I cried. "I have it. I will help you. Can you do housework?"

"Why, yes, Miss, I suppose so," she answered, with wondering eyes.

"Then fix yourself up a little and come with me. I will give you a place as housemaid in my home. What you don't know, you will soon learn. You shall have a nice clean bedroom, with plenty to eat, print dresses in the morning, black stuff in the afternoon, with white caps and aprons, and collars and cuffs. I will buy them for you as we go along. We will pay you £16 a year to commence. Come, why don't you get your things on? We will settle up the back rent and return the sewing-machine to the instalment people."

The girl had risen from her chair and, to my astonishment, confronted me angrily, her cheeks aflame and her eyes blazing.

"Did you come only to insult me?" she demanded, stamping her feet. "I go out to service! I wear caps and aprons, those badges of slavery! No, thank you. I prefer to keep my liberty and be independent."

What was she talking about? Her liberty, her independence? I was bewildered, and could scarcely believe my ears. I had been so interested in this girl, and for the past two months had vainly tried to think of a plan whereby I could help her. I knew she was poor and proud, and would not take a penny from me unless she felt she had earned it. I had finally decided to give her a comfortable situation in my own home, and this was the way she received my suggestion. She had deemed my offer an insult. So this was the outcome of my maiden effort in the missionary line! She had asked for bread, and I, according to her way of thinking, had proffered her a stone. Disconsolate and disappointed, I left her, and in my bitterness was half resolved to steel my heart for ever against the woes of my own sex, and never again venture outside the legitimate paths of journalism.

However, my cynical resolution was not carried

B 2

out, for the following day I was seized with a womanly curiosity to learn something more about this wonderful "liberty" the sewing girl seemed to value so highly; and, with that in view, I passed considerable time among the working women of London, trying to gain a clue to the meaning of their war-cry, "Independence." Everywhere I heard that word. It sounded above the clickety-clack of the type-writer while the fingers flew over the keys; the noisily-turning factory-wheels failed to drown it; I heard it over the clink of the barmaid's glasses; it mingled with the ring of the telephone-bell, the whirr of the cash-machine, and the refrain of the chorus-girl. The telegraph-operator murmured the word as she took down the letters of the various messages, the schoolmistress whispered it as she gave out the morrow's lesson in arithmetic, the female book-keeper uttered it while she added up the long column of figures. Even the little sub-editress, earning a salary of £1 a week for stealing copy from the daily journals, seemed imbued with that so-called "spirit of independence." "Give me my liberty and independence!" That was the burden of their song. Some of them belonged to "The Independent Young Ladies' League," some to a "Liberty Club," others to "The Society for Promoting the Equality of Classes," and the rest were members of various societies and orders with similar names, while all prated of liberty and freedom like Young America just let loose.

Their ideas seemed to be vague and wandering, and the majority of them were hardly able to give a proper definition of the word they used so glibly.

They were not a cheerful lot of girls by any means. Indeed, their solitary happiness was apparently in the belief that they were independent. Some of them were what are generally termed "ladies by birth," others were ladies by education. Each individual girl rejoiced in the appellation "young lady," whether she were a visiting governess or a clerk in a tobacco shop. They worked early and late at their professions and trades, and their salaries varied from 6s. to 30s. a week. They supported themselves, and often had several younger brothers and sisters dependent upon them. Week after week, month after month, and year after year, they had toiled with little advancement or encouragement. Most of them belonged to the commonplace order, neither clever nor stupid, only ordinary, everyday young women, working for their living.

Many were hungry, some were badly clothed, few had comfortable beds or clean lodgings. A number of them had porridge for breakfast and watercress for supper, with no midday meal. One young woman assured me that boiled rice was her perpetual diet, and that, while it was filling, it became tiresome in the long run. But, despite these numerous inconveniences, they were all "independent" girls, every one of them. Several times I broached the subject of domestic service as a possible release from their troubles, but they laughed me to scorn and flaunted the flag of liberty in my face. What! go to service? Not they! Why, they could only have one night off each week, and no followers. Besides, who could wear caps and aprons without despising herself?

I began to wonder if there really could be anything terrible connected with domestic service which should make these poor girls so shrink from it. For myself, I knew little or nothing about housework, but the belief that there was nothing incompatible between gentility and domestic work had always been a hobby of mine. Why could not a refined English girl wash dishes, make beds, and roast a leg of mutton just as well as a member of the lower classes? Wherein would she demean herself by doing this work and receiving wages for the same?

But there were the caps and aprons. Could an educated girl wear them without diminishing her self-respect? Why was not a housemaid's cap just as respectable as that worn by a "lady nurse"? For my own part, I had always insisted that no Paris milliner could manufacture any headgear more becoming to the majority of women than the white ruffled cap of the domestic servant employed by members of the upper classes. A pretty maid, to my mind, was much prettier with a cap than without one, while the face of an ugly girl was also improved by it. But these "slavery badges," I was told, were not the only bugbears of the servant-girl.

I had a curiosity to find out just what these trials were, and to discover why this service was looked upon with so much contumely. As a mistress, however kind and considerate I might be, it was impossible for me to get a perfect understanding of the inner working of the household machinery. There was only one way to get at the root of the matter, and that was to go out to service myself.

I arrived at this decision one morning in the latter part of August, and I no sooner decided than I

began to make preparations for my campaign. I
first purchased some goods for a print dress, which I
had made up in the prevailing style for housemaids,
together with a black serge gown for afternoon wear.
Then I bought three linen aprons for morning, and
as many fine muslin ones for dress-up occasions.
They were prettily trimmed with embroidery, and
the ruffled epaulettes were a joy to behold. Cuffs and
collars and caps with long streamers completed my
outfit. Then I hired a room in Camberwell for 2s. 6d.
a week, where I might have letters addressed, and
arrangements were made with a titled friend to give
me a reference as to respectability and honesty.

Until all these details were settled, I gave little
thought as to how I should get the situation I desired,
nor the difficulties I should be likely to encounter. I
had a nineteenth-century woman's confidence in my
ability to accomplish whatever I should set out to do,
and the remembrance of my first and only attempt
at sweeping a floor (which left me with blistered
hands) did not in the least daunt my spirit. I should
never have been tempted to call myself a domesticated woman, and my experiences in household duties,
so far as the actual work might be concerned, was
very limited; yet I prided myself upon my abilities
in the "knowing how" line. If I had never washed
dishes, I knew how they ought to be done; and I
was thoroughly convinced that dish-washing, sweeping, dusting, making beds, and "turning out" rooms,
could be reduced—or, rather, elevated—to a science.
I felt sure that in all kinds of work there were hard
methods and easy ones. By going out to service I
should discover which was which, and then I should

be able to write a series of articles on "Housework Made Easy," thus benefiting womankind in general and servant-girls in particular.

In order to inform myself as to just where my valuable services were required, I picked up the morning paper and looked among the "Situations Vacant."

WANTED.—Housemaid where Parlourmaid is kept; must be neat, of good appearance, tall, and thoroughly capable, with at least twelve months' character.

It was evident that I would not suit that advertiser, for I was not tall, neither was I possessed of a twelve-months' character. I proceeded down the column, and to my utter dismay I found that length of body, as well as length of character, was considered indispensable in a housemaid or parlourmaid. There were several places open to "generals," but most of them were required to look after the babies, besides doing the other work, and I felt unequal to the task. Cooks were in great demand, but they also must needs have long characters.

Still, I did not lose heart, but bearing in mind the motto of the Americans, "Trust in the Lord and advertise," I wrote out an advertisement and took it to a newspaper office in Fleet Street. As I handed it to the receiving clerk, I observed that a puzzled look overspread his features. My notice was apparently something of a novelty to him, for, after re-reading it, he took it across the room to another clerk, who, when he had read it, smiled, and said, "It's all right. Put it in." The next morning—August 23rd

—there appeared in the columns of "Situations Wanted" the following :—

A S Housemaid, Parlourmaid, or House-Parlourmaid. —A refined and educated young woman, obliged to earn her living, and unable to find other employment, wants situation as above. Expects only such treatment as is given to servants. Will wear caps and aprons, but would not wish to share bed with another. Thoroughly reliable and competent. References ; town or country. Wages, £14.—Address ——.

CHAPTER II.

SEEKING A SITUATION.

THE day after my advertisement appeared I received 159 letters and postcards in reply. This was encouraging, for it proved conclusively that the demand for good servants was much greater than the supply, and also that there could not be any firmly-rooted objection to educated domestic help. Several of the writers wanted "lady-helps" and assured me that I should have nothing to do in the way of "menial service." A Southampton lady required a thoroughly educated young person for children, and said she had been advertising for a lady nurse. But it was not my object to go out as a lady-help, or a nurse. I wished a situation as an ordinary servant. One inquisitive person demanded to know my age, height, position in life, my father's business, if my mother was a gentlewoman, and whether I was a Churchwoman or a Dissenter—most of which information seemed to me not at all relevant to the subject in hand. An old lady of seventy wanted

someone nice and quiet, with a restful appearance,
for a parlourmaid, because she had rheumatism so
badly and would like her knees rubbed. A lodging-
house keeper was in need of a young woman who
would study her interest, and answer board and
residence advertisements in the papers. One of the
latter class wrote :

"Seeing your advertisement in the morning paper,
wanting a home and friendship of a friend, I want a
young person to assist me in the up-stairs duties of a
first-class lodging-house, to look after and see and
do all that is necessary, and take entire care and
responsibility of the same. You would have to wear
caps and aprons of course, when anyone was in the
house, but not otherwise ; and I would do anything
for your comfort if only you would study me. I
have a young daughter of my own, but she prefers
to go to business, and will not work in the house,
and I want you to take her place."

All this was very flattering, and showed the esteem
in which the lady held me ; but I felt that the entire
care and responsibility of a lodging-house, besides
the duty of being a daughter to anybody, would be
too great a weight on my shoulders.

Another writer assured me that I should find her
a considerate mistress, and said that she had always
been told that she spoiled her maids by considering
them too much, which, she began to think, was true.
Many offered higher wages than those I had asked
for, and a few thought my terms too high, on account
of my probable inexperience. A young matron at
Clapham Common was sure I should suit her. I
would have the house-work to do and must mind a

five-months' baby. If I was a nice person, I would be happy in the situation. She could not give over £12. The number of women with babies to mind seemed very numerous. The wife of a colonel wished to know if I would do the pocket-handkerchiefs and stockings each week for herself and three daughters, besides attending to the known duties of a house-parlourmaid. Somehow, I was convinced that this was more than I ought to undertake. Mrs. Black, of Hyde Park Gate, required a housemaid who must be a good dressmaker. She requested my photo with full particulars. No agent need apply. Windows and a little washing to be done. (Did Mrs. Black forget that there is a law against allowing women-servants to wash windows?) Mrs. Smith, living near Oxford Circus, wanted a trustworthy, reliable, clean girl to do the work of a private house. She had a domesticated daughter, three sons and a husband, and would want the washing done at home. Wages £10, or £12 with no beer. Just where the clothes would be dried after the washing was done at home was a source of conjecture in my mind, and I doubted my ability to put a proper gloss on the shirt-fronts of the three sons and the husband.

Kind and thoughtful letters were numerous. Mrs Burns, living in a flat near Portland Place, wrote that she desired a house-parlourmaid who, in conjunction with the cook, would do the work of the flat. I could have a separate bedroom, and she would do everything in her power to make me feel that I was not without friends and home. A very nice letter came from Thames Ditton, which ended by saying "If you think my situation at all what you are seeking, will you give me some references? and, as I am a stranger to you, I will send references in return." This was the only instance in which the employer spoke of giving references, although I was always required to furnish them. Just why a "character" should be demanded on one side only is beyond my comprehension. Why should not the give-and-take plan be followed in such cases? Is not a mistress likely to prove as unmanageable as a servant?

An enterprising City man wrote that he was looking out for a young lady who would invest capital to build up a toy trade in a neighbourhood where there was no opposition. He would be pleased to hear if I was disposed to come to terms. Then I opened a letter couched in this language :—

DEAR MISS,—Seeing your advertisement, I am moved to write and say that I admire your pluck and am glad to know there is at least one young woman with sense enough to see that there is no disgrace in domestic labour. I would like to marry a girl like you, if you are not too old or ugly, which I do not believe you are. Please state age, complexion, height, temperament, and personal appearance, and tell me if you would accept for a husband an honest mechanic, aged 28, and earning £200 a year. If so, give me your address, and I will come and see you with all honourable intentions. It is much better for a girl like you to be married and have a protector than to be a housemaid.

In my opinion, the writer of that epistle is a prize in the matrimonial market, and I should be glad to give his name and address to any young woman who can answer his requirements and thinks she would be able to appreciate the situation.

There were several replies from bachelors and widowers wanting " companion-working-lady-housekeepers." They all assured me that there was very little work to be done. Mr. Alexander Macfarlane, of Glasgow, wished for particulars in regard to age, experience, and qualifications for his situation as house-parlourmaid. He stated that he was a single gentleman, whose establishment consisted of cook-housekeeper, kitchenmaid, and house-parlourmaid— all English. Each servant had a separate room. He desired to know if I had any experience in valeting, if I understood lamps, and how my knowledge of silver-cleaning and waiting at table had been gained. I must give particulars as to last two situations, and reasons for leaving them. What allowance would I require in addition to wages for finding myself in beer, tea, sugar, and washing? He requested my photograph, which he would return at once, and, if appearance and qualifications were satisfactory, he would arrange for an interview.

In spite of Mr. Macfarlane's insinuation that I might need an extra allowance for beer-money, I conceived the greatest admiration for him, because he was the only man who took me at my word, and offered me a place as a regular servant. In reply, I wrote him some particulars, stating that I was a teetotaller, had never been out to service, and could only give reference as regarded my respectability and honesty, but felt competent to undertake the work he mentioned, including the valeting. His answer was straightforward. He feared that a young woman of my bringing up and education would not find it pleasant to work in his house under the supervision of a cook-housekeeper. It would be better for me to go in a small family where there was a lady at the head of the household. If he heard of any place he thought suitable for me, he would write immediately, as he felt interested in me and desired to help me.

Would that there were more Alexander Macfarlanes in the world !

About half the letters contained stamps for reply, and I conscientiously wrote to every person who enclosed a stamp. The story I told of my circumstances was a simple one and as near the truth as I thought politic to make it. I was an orphan and almost alone in London, well educated, but my education was such as did not fit me for anything in particular. I could not obtain employment in the City, as I did not write a good hand, and, not understanding the languages or music, found it difficult to get a position as governess. Nothing was left me but domestic work, which I understood perfectly. I thought it no disgrace to be in service, and had determined to get a place as housemaid or parlourmaid, asking no favours and desiring only wages for services rendered. I gave the Camberwell address, and signed my letters Elizabeth Barrows. In some cases I received no answers, but about fifty appointments were made for me to call in various parts of London. Mrs. Clifford-Morris, who was spending a few weeks in Brighton, asked me to call on her husband, a solicitor, in Chancery Lane, who could then give her particulars in regard to me. She thought she could employ me as useful help in her flat when she returned home. In her several letters she addressed me as "My dear Miss Barrows," and the sympathetic, delicate manner in which she treated me quite won my heart. I did not call on Mr. Clifford-Morris, as I felt that to enter the service of his wife, knowing that I should remain only a short time, might put her to inconvenience in her household arrangements for the winter and be but small return for her kindness to me. Yet I determined to try to find her such a person as she wanted, and I still hope that I may be able to send her someone who would appreciate the home she has to offer.

On the morning of Friday, September 1, I started out in answer to some of the appointments made for that day. My first call was on a Miss Martin, who was at the head of what she described as a "high-class private hotel" in Mayfair. The man-servant who admitted me, asked me into the drawing-room, but, realising that henceforth I could no longer lay claim to the title of "young lady," but must consider myself only in the light of a "young person," I thought perhaps it would be better for me to remain in the hall, so I sat down on the hat-rack in orthodox servant-girl fashion, and tried to compose myself for the interview. Miss Martin, a pleasant-faced spinster of about forty, soon made her appearance, and asked me up to the drawing-room. She led me to a window, looked me over, and then shook her head, kindly but firmly.

"My dear, you are too little!" was her first exclamation.

"But I am strong, neat, willing, respectable, &c." I insisted. "Please do not despise me because I am small."

Miss Martin still looked doubtful; then she commenced to tell me of all the work a housemaid would be expected to do, and afterwards showed me through the house, with a view of discouraging me. I felt that I must say something to convince her of my capabilities, so I ventured to suggest that I could dust the chairs in a much better way than they had been done, and explained to her a new and improved method of making beds. I also informed her that I was able to remove the numerous candle-grease spots with which the carpets were sprinkled, by the application of brown paper and a hot flat-iron to the injured parts. Miss Martin's face began to light up, and I could see I was making an impression. I went on and discussed learnedly the proper way to polish looking-glasses and shine the tiled fireplaces, while her enthusiasm increased. When I was leaving I gave her the name of my reference, and she promised to write me her decision. What was my disappointment that evening to receive a letter saying she had not written to the reference as she could not help thinking I was too small and delicate to do the work! It seemed that, as soon as my inspiring presence had vanished, she remembered only my diminutive stature.

From Mayfair I went to Grosvenor Square, and met a most formidable-looking lady of the house. She did not ask me to sit down, but commenced at once to read me off a list of the duties to be performed by the parlourmaid, when, suddenly giving me a very scrutinising look, she advanced towards me, and lifting her hand warningly, ejaculated, " No fringe allowed!" I sprang back, and instinctively put my hand to my forehead as a protection, fearing she might brandish a pair of scissors before me and barber me then and there. What! put back my fringe! I had entirely overlooked the fact that many servants were not allowed to wear a fringe.

"I couldn't part with it, ma'am," I answered in humble and trembling accents. Then I made a frightened retreat, and walked in the direction of

"NO FRINGE ALLOWED!"

Regent's Park. No fringe, indeed! Was it possible that one of my own sex could be so cruel as to wish to deprive me of my halo? Besides, my caps were not becoming without a fringe. Liberty! Independence! I began more fully to understand the meaning of the words, and I wondered if, after all, I should not end by joining "The Independent Young Ladies' League."

I rang the bell of a large house in Marylebone Road, and was admitted to the presence of Mrs.

C

Green, who had wired me to call that morning. She was an elderly woman, tall and stately, with a kind face which quite reassured me. She asked me to sit down and then to stand up.

"I am afraid you will not do. You are so short. You see, a parlourmaid must have long arms in order to reach things on the table, and a housemaid should also be tall ; else how can she put the linen away on the top shelves and wash the looking-glasses in the drawing-room ? Why do you not try to get a place as nurserymaid or governess to small children ?"

I did not feel at liberty to say just why I did not do this. I only said that I knew so little about children that I was afraid to undertake so great a responsibility.

"Well," said she, "you would not suit for my house—the work is too hard for you—yet I must try to help you. It is so sad for a girl to be alone in this great city. I was just eating my luncheon. Will you have a nice chop and cup of tea? In the meantime I will see what I can do for you."

I was not hungry, but I went with her to the dining-room while she finished her meal, and answered as truthfully as I could the questions she put concerning myself.

"Can you sew ?" she asked.

My thoughts turned involuntarily to the many times I had tried to learn the art of needlework, which had resulted only in pricked fingers and a bad temper. Once I remembered to have been able to get through a little patchwork. Dared I say that I could sew? Then I answered, "Yes, ma'am, a little," inwardly praying that she might never discover how very little that "little" was. She went to her desk, wrote a note, and handed it to me sealed. "This is a letter to a friend of mine in South Kensington, a lady who keeps a high-class employment agency. Go to her this afternoon, and she may be able to get you more congenial work than that of an ordinary servant. Take the Underground. Here is your fare."

To my horror she slipped a half-crown piece into my hand. I protested that I had a little money, and could not think of taking it, but she insisted, and I felt I could not refuse it without exciting her suspicion. "Good-bye. Write me how you get along. I shall always be interested in you," and with a motherly pat on the head she dismissed me. I wandered along Marylebone Road with the letter and the money, feeling like a culprit. Might I not be arrested on the charge of obtaining money under false pretences? Would the excuse that I was a journalist, doing evil that good might come, protect me from the law? The coin almost burned a hole into my glove. Just then a woman, grinding a small organ, passed me, and I thrust the money into her hand and rushed away before she could overwhelm me with thanks. I broke the seal of the letter, and read :—

DEAR MRS. ——,—The bearer interests me. Her case seems a sad one. Can you advise her how to get work? I know you won't mind the trouble of doing anyone a kindness. She seems so forlorn, alone in a large city.

God forbid that I should ever grow pessimistic, and think womankind cold and heartless, when such

C 2

women as Mrs. Green live in the world! Surely, future generations of working girls will rise up to call her blessed!

I spent a week in my search for a situation. Among the people I met, a Thackeray or a Dickens would have found abundant material for many characters in many books. I called on bachelors, widowers and widows, ladies of title, members of the upper and middle classes, actresses, literary women, and boarding-house keepers. They all agreed that it was the proper thing for educated girls to go out to service, and that a great change must be brought about in the class of domestics to be employed. However, the majority of them found some objection to giving me a trial. A woman on Cambridge Terrace offered me a place as parlourmaid in a house where twenty lodgers were taken, and I would have accepted it but for the fear that at the end of the week's trial she was to give me I would be too much reduced in flesh and spirit to linger long on the earth, for each of the twenty lodgers must have his or her meals carried up-stairs on a tray. Another boarding-house keeper was so sorry I had not £100 to invest in the business, as she would have liked to have taken me into partnership. In Gloucester Road a Mrs. Weldon, living in a small house, with only herself and husband in family, said she liked my appearance and manner, but that I did not give her enough particulars concerning my private history and family affairs. I thought her suspicious manner of treating me far from delicate, especially as I gave her the name of a well-known London lady as reference, who, I informed her, had known me from childhood. Had I been an ordinary applicant for a situation, I should have attempted to give her a lesson in politeness and considerateness for the feelings of others. It is neither consistent nor just that a young woman applying for a place as servant should be subjected to such a catechism as that through which this woman put me. It is quite as honourable for servants to listen at keyholes as for mistresses to attempt this prying into personal secrets.

At last I found an engagement. Mrs. Allison, residing in a large house in the neighbourhood of Portman Square, wrote to inform me that my reference was satisfactory, and she would give me a place as housemaid. She ended by saying—

"I think I shall be able to smooth over many of the rough places for you, and give you a comfortable home."

She would expect me on the evening of September 14. During the interval I made a close study of a little book entitled "Servants' Duties' and endeavoured to make myself proficient in all that pertained to my chosen work. I became quite an expert in the use of the words "ma'am" and "sir." At the appointed time I presented myself and my handbag at the door of the Portman Square mansion, ready to enter my first situation as housemaid.

CHAPTER III.

"ELIZABETH BARROWS," HOUSEMAID.

MY ring at Mrs. Allison's door-bell was answered by the parlourmaid, who, without any explanations on my part, seemed at once to recognise me as a co-labourer, and led me to the servants' room on the fifth floor. I was immediately struck with the cheerless and comfortless aspect of the place where I was to sleep and, perchance, to dream for a week or longer. Three iron bedsteads stood in a row, and in front of each was a strip of ragged carpet. There were two chairs, a green chest of drawers, with a rickety-looking-glass on top, and two green washstands, with two bowls and pitchers. When I saw these latter articles, it occurred to me that I had been told three servants were to occupy the room, and I began to wonder whether I would be obliged to share my washbasin with the cook or the parlourmaid. I did not like the prospect of such a contingency, and I was far from being convinced of the truth of the saying that "whatever is, is right." Still, I was philosophical enough to understand that, whatever must be, must be, and I commenced to unpack my few belongings. Annie, the parlourmaid, had indicated the drawer in the green chest which was to be my individual property, so I put away my caps, aprons, collars, cuffs, and the blue print dress I was to don the next morning. Over the mantel hung a brightly-coloured motto. It read, "Whatsoever thy hand findeth to do, do it with thy might." The verse was very *à propos* and inspired fresh courage in my trembling heart as I tied on my prettiest apron and went to the glass to adjust my cap. Then, after a final satisfactory glance into the mirror, I descended to Mrs. Allison's sitting-room on the second floor. I found that lady dusting the various ornaments on her writing-desk with a yellow silk duster.

She smiled propitiously upon me, and said, "Good-evening, Elizabeth. Go right down to the kitchen. Annie will tell you about the work."

"Yes, ma'am," I replied; "but please call me Lizzie I like it better."

"Very well, Lizzie."

That was the extent of our conversation. Mrs. Allison had no words to waste on her servants. Indeed, I was glad of it. When I had first called on her, she listened respectfully to the story I had to tell, took its truthfulness for granted, and said she would do the same thing in my circumstances. She asked no unnecessary questions, and I was prepared to like her because she had not attempted to pry into my family secrets nor to deprive me of my fringe. I had explained to her that, although I might be above the ordinary servant in education and bringing up, I did not wish it to make any difference in her treatment of me. In this matter she had respected my wishes, and I felt that I was in a fair way to find out just what were her relations with the young women who were employed in her household in the capacity of domestic helps.

In the kitchen I found Annie standing before the fire grilling mutton chops. She explained that a new cook would be there the following Monday, and that she was to prepare the meals until then. Eyeing me critically, she exclaimed, "Did she tell you to wear caps with streamers?" I guessed that "she" referred to the mistress of the house, and informed her that I was wearing streamers on my own responsibility. She thought my style was much prettier than her own French caps, and declared her intention of purchasing some like mine.

"Been out to service before?" was her next inquiry.

"No; this is my first place."

"You'll find it's not so easy as it looks," she remarked, with a very superior and knowing air. "We're on board wages till the cook comes," she continued. "There's your allowance on the shelf."

I remembered that at home some of our own servants had often referred enthusiastically to certain times when they had been put on board wages and the money they had been able to lay by at the end of the week. I walked with elastic steps towards the shelf to which Annie pointed, and picked up 1s. 6d. Then my hopes went down about 90 degrees in the shade.

"Is this to buy breakfast?" I asked.

Annie tittered.

"Well, I should say it was to buy breakfast, dinner, supper, and afternoon tea," was her announcement.

Who would have believed it? To be sure, I had never sat down and calculated to a nicety just the quantity of eatables 1s. 6d. would buy; but still I doubted my ability to make it go that far, especially when I learned that pepper, salt, mustard, vinegar, and sugar were also included in the meals. I began to have great respect for that 1s. 6d.

I saw that Annie was inclined to be friendly, which was a source of great satisfaction to me, for I knew there must exist a spirit of *camaraderie* between myself and fellow-servants, else I should never be able to accomplish what I had set out to do—that is, discover the ins and outs of domestic service. I was

"ELIZABETH BARROWS," HOUSEMAID.

(From a Photograph by the London Stereoscopic Company.)

fully prepared to enter into the joys and sorrows of
the kitchen, and with that in view I tried to be as
agreeable as possible to Annie. She had noticed
nothing peculiar about me, with the exception of
streamers. If my manner of speech was different from
hers, she did not observe it, but took me for one of her
own kind. Annie's attitude toward me was not in
any way intended to add to my self-conceit, and any
intellectual bearing I might have thought I possessed
did not apparently show up to advantage in the garb
of cap and apron.

Later in the evening we made the round of the
rooms. Annie gave me explicit instructions as to how
to tidy them up, turn down the beds and make the
washstands ready for use. When this work was done,
I was more tired than I had ever been in my life.
What with emptying out the washbowls and refilling
the pitchers, I had gone up and down two flights of
stairs eight times, carrying heavy water-cans and pails.
To the kitchen we again descended, and, while I wiped
the dishes, Annie entertained me by telling me something of the family with whom I was to live. There
were Mr. and Mrs. Allison, three daughters, and two
sons. Two of the young ladies were at the seaside,
and would return with their maid on Saturday. The
staff of servants included cook, parlourmaid, housemaid, and ladies' maid. Annie had formerly been
housemaid in the family where she was now parlourmaid, so she was able to instruct me as to my duties.
She opened a little cupboard off the kitchen and
brought out a basket of underwear and stockings.
It was the housemaid's basket, and I was to spend my
evenings in attending to the mending. I looked

aghast at the contents. How should I, with my slight knowledge of needlework, attempt to darn the woollen socks of the gentlemen of the house? Just then Annie was called to the hall to answer the whistle of the speaking-tube, and returned to say that Mrs. Allison would see me in the study and give me a list of the work I was to do the following day. I welcomed this news as a present deliverance from the mending problem, but when I got that list from Mrs. Allison, I felt that my doom was sealed. It seemed to me that the responsibilities put upon my shoulders were tremendous.

I was to rise at six in the morning, and my first duty was to shake and brush Mr. Allison's trousers, which I would find hanging on the doorknob outside his room. I was about to inform Mrs. Allison that I did not engage as a valet, and was not up in the art of brushing trousers, when I suddenly remembered that I was not a "young lady" now, but a "young person," expected to do with her might whatever her hands found to do. Did not the motto in my bedroom so inform me? I made no remarks, and listened for the second duty, which was to brush Mrs. Allison's dress and carry all the boots to the kitchen for Annie to polish. I was glad of the latter clause, for, had I been told to shine the boots, I think I should have despaired. Afterwards I would sweep and dust four flights of stairs and five halls, clean up and dust the study and drawing-rooms, and carry a can of hot water to each person, knocking on the door to wake him or her up. I concluded that when I had accomplished all these things, I should have done a good day's work; but were my ears deceiving me? What was Mrs. Allison saying?

"Then you may eat your breakfast!"

So I was to achieve all those Herculean feats on an empty stomach! Well, if that was the case, I certainly ought to be able to perform wonders after I had breakfasted.

Mrs. Allison continued with her list, never noting my perturbed countenance.

"After you have breakfasted, Lizzie, you must help Annie with the dishes, then make the beds, clean up the washstands, fill the water-jugs, sweep and dust the bedrooms, attend to the candlesticks, and put everything in perfect order in the sitting-rooms. You will get this done by eleven o'clock." (On that point I was tempted to contradict her flatly, but I knew discretion was the better part of valour, and preserved silence.) "From eleven till three," went on my mistress, "you will turn out one or two of the rooms and eat your dinner in the meantime. At four o'clock I want you to be dressed with clean cap and apron. Then you will get the servants' afternoon tea and clear it away, and you can fill up the time until supper with needlework." (That needlework still relentlessly pursued me.) After supper I was to make the round of the rooms again and sew until a quarter-past ten. Then I might go to bed, a consummation devoutly to be wished for!

After hearing the "list," I bowed politely to Mrs. Allison, said, "Very well, ma'am," and joined Annie in the kitchen. She greeted me with a fiendish grin, and said, "Did she say anything about the scrubbing?"

"Scrubbing! Must I scrub?" I almost shrieked.

"You'll think so, when you get at it! Why, you have to scrub a bedroom all over every day, and sometimes two! You see, you must turn out a room each day, and there's no carpet on the bedrooms; only a narrow rug before the bed. On turning out day, you must shake the rug and scrub up the floor and the paint. It do make your hands and arms ache, I tell you. It's too bad you took such a hard place for your first time in service!"

She said this rather pityingly. No wonder! I pitied myself. It was ten o'clock.

"Come," said I, "let us go to bed. I'm so tired!"

Annie laughed.

"Well, you're a greeny, sure enough! When you're in service, you can't go to bed when you like. Master Tom is out, and hasn't a key. We'll have to let him in. You might do some needlework while we're waiting."

That was the last straw that broke the camel's back. I put my head down on the kitchen table and silently wept.

At eleven o'clock Master Tom came in, and we went to our bedroom. I noted that the bed had neither springs nor hair mattress, but I slept, nevertheless, and all night long in my dreams came visions of much-worn scrubbing-brushes and basket upon basket of gentlemen's undarned socks. Suddenly I heard a loud noise like the clanking of a cow-bell. I jumped up, and went to Annie's bed to demand the meaning of the horrible racket.

"Why, it's six o'clock; that's all. The missus has an alarm-bell connected with her room. She sends it off every morning to make us get up."

I was dressed in an instant, and with my written list in hand, started off to attend to order number one. The trousers and the dress were duly brushed, the stairs and halls swept and dusted, and each person supplied with a hot-water can. Then I went into the study, which was a large room. There were dozens of ornaments on the desk and mantel, which it seemed an endless task to dust and rearrange. My head ached for the want of food, yet I knew that I had not only the study to finish, but two large drawing-rooms to attend to. I noticed that the drawing rooms and the study were the only really cheerful rooms in the house. All the comforts and pictures and ornaments were crowded together in these rooms, and to do them up properly was no easy piece of work, but they were on the list to be done before breakfast. At 8.30 I had finished them, however, and went to the kitchen.

Annie informed me that the servants' cupboard was in a veritable Mother Hubbard state, and, if I wanted anything for breakfast besides tea and bread, I must go and buy it. I took my 1s. 6d. and went out to shop, and, remembering that my own home was only a short distance from the place where I was "in service," I ran around there and filled my basket with provisions, while my 1s. 6d. remained intact. Annie's face beamed when she saw the wonderful purchases I had effected, all with 1s. 6d., and I then and there established the reputation of being a good provider. She insisted that she must share the expense, and wished to know the price of each article, which I gave her as follows :—One pound of strawberry jam (whole berries), 2d. per pound; two pounds of best mutton chops, 6d.; three pounds of fresh tomatoes, 3d. for the lot; four rashers best streaked bacon, ½d. per rasher; large piece of beef for roasting, 5d. Annie declared she never knew you could buy things so cheap, and wanted the addresses of the shops I patronised. It is unnecessary to say that I had forgotten their location, and it is also needless to explain that from that time, until the cook came, I was delegated to do the marketing and hunt up these daily bargains, much to the diminishing of the contents of the larder at home. That morning we breakfasted off mutton chops and tomato sauce, while the family up-stairs were content to start the day with one egg each and a slice of toast.

That first day "in service" lingers in my memory as a sort of nightmare. The whole house seemed arranged in such a way as to make the work as hard as possible. The bath-room was on the top floor, and, as all the water must be carried from there to the bedrooms below, it was no small matter to fill the water-pitchers. Then, in washing, every member of the family seemed to have taken particular pains to spill as much water about as possible, and everything had to be removed from the washstands before they could be put in order. All this might have been prevented had the bowls been filled not quite so full and a little care been exercised. Everything was thrown down where it had been used, though it was just as easy to return these various articles to their proper places. The linen cupboard in Mrs. Allison's room was guarded by an immense couch, on which were piled dozens of boxes containing dresses, which must all be removed before I could get fresh towels. Then the couch had to

be pushed back again, and the boxes heaped on top.
All the bedrooms were gloomy and devoid of comfort, to say nothing of ornaments. The floors, as
Annie had informed me, were not carpeted, and
served to bring forcibly to my mind the scrubbing
I should have to do. Eleven o'clock came, and I
had not finished the bedroom work. There were all
the candlesticks to scrape off. One of them, a handsome bronze figure of Minerva, it took me just one
hour to get clean. The armour, draperies, and petti-
coats of the goddess were plentifully sprinkled with
candle-grease, which soap and water failed to eradi-
cate, so there was nothing to do but scrape it off
with a hair-pin, all of which took much valuable
time. "What, an hour spent in cleaning a candle-
stick!" some sensible housewife may exclaim. I
can only tell her to get a bronze Minerva and see
if she can do it in quicker time.

At half-past one Annie and I were eating dinner,
when a whistle sounded through the speaking-tube.

"Yes, ma'am," I called, ready to take Mrs. Allison's order.

"Lizzie, you did not close the schoolroom window.
Come up and attend to it."

I went to the schoolroom, on the top floor; it
was five flights from the kitchen. The lady of the
house sat at a table reading a magazine. I closed
the window and went down to finish my dinner.

This was an instance of the way Mrs. Allison tried
to "smooth over the rough places" for me and make
my situation as comfortable as possible.

CHAPTER IV.

ROUGH PLACES "SMOOTHED OVER."

WHEN I had spent two days in Mrs. Allison's service, I began to wonder what the "rough places" would have been like had she not attempted to smooth them over. She certainly could not have accused me of being a slow worker, and I did not "dilly-dally" over my duties, yet on Friday and Saturday I found it impossible to make time for "turning out" the rooms, however much I hurried. I no sooner finished tidying up the bedrooms than the washbowls were again filled to overflowing with soapy water and needed further attention. When I had brushed one dress and hung it in the wardrobe, another flannel gown or coat would be hung out on the banisters. "Such little things!" someone may say. Yes, that is true. A dress may be brushed in five minutes, and a washbasin emptied and wiped out in less time, but these small things call a servant away from her more important work and put her behind for the whole day. On Saturday morning, when I was washing out the dusters in the housemaid's cupboard, Mrs. Allison presented me with a pair of her husband's old kid-gloves, saying they would be "nice to wear when brushing the grates." I uttered a silent prayer that the cold days might not come during my stay, and put them away for the use of my successor. The carrying of coals,

D

building of fires, and emptying ashes are doubtless
the hardest part of the work which falls to the
women servants in a house where no man is kept,
especially in families where every member insists
on being comfortable and having fires in the bedrooms. However, Annie informed me that at Mrs.
Allison's the bedrooms were not heated in the winter.
Still, with each sleeping-room there was connected
a sitting-room, where fires were kept, besides two
grates in the drawing-rooms; all of which work fell
to the lot of the housemaid.

I soon became accustomed to my work, and was
really surprised at the readiness with which I put
into practice all I learned from my little book on
" Servants' Duties," and, although I knew my stay
was only a temporary one, I interested myself to
discover the easiest and quickest ways for doing the
work. After sweeping the stairs the first morning,
I found that the small banister brush used for that
purpose in most London houses was not a convenient
or suitable implement, as it was impossible to get
into the corners with it, so it was necessary to use
two brushes in the operation. I felt sure that a
whisk broom would better meet my requirements,
and requested Mrs. Allison to get me one; but she
was not inclined to give any help in the way of
labour-saving appliances, so I used my own little
broom which I had taken with me for brushing my
coat. After that the corners were beautifully clean.
I would recommend this sort of brush to all housekeepers, not only because of its easy application to
the corners, but for the reason that there is no
awkward, heavy piece of wood about it, making that

disagreeable knockety-knock every time a step is
brushed, thus saving wear and tear on the nerves
of the housemaid and allowing the members of the
family to continue their morning sleep undisturbed
by the racket. In the same way, for sweeping both
bare floors and carpets, the long-handled straight
broom, known as the "American broom," seems
to me to be ever so much more convenient and
easy to manipulate than the English brush broom,
which, like the banister broom, will not go into the
corners.

All the stairs of the house were covered with felt,
the hardest floor-covering in the world to keep clean.
Besides the daily sweeping, I was obliged to rub them
frequently with a damp cloth in order to remove the
accumulated dust and lint. The halls and passages
were of stone, with rugs scattered about, which proved
to be perfect traps for dust and dirt, and showed conclusively that properly carpeted halls were, in the
long run, a great saving of labour. There were gas-
pipes in every room, needing only the addition of
fixtures to make them ready for use, and thus
dispense with the numerous candlesticks that were
to be refilled every day. In the halls, on the stairs,
and in every room of the house, from the kitchen to
the fifth floor, candle-grease was plentifully sprinkled,
and my brown paper and hot flat-iron were in constant demand.

It seemed to me that, by expending a little
thought and money, a vast amount of unnecessary
time might be saved as regarded the continual tidying
up of bedrooms, &c. For instance, why should beds
first be made up with the blankets and coverlets over

D 2

the pillows, and then partly remade in the evening when the beds are "turned down"? An easier and much neater way would be to turn down the sheets at once and place the pillows on the outside. Thus only one handling is necessary.

If mistresses would devote more thought to this saving of labour, they would find they were at the same time lessening their household expenses by preventing an unnecessary outlay in servants' wages, for where work is made light, and quick methods employed, fewer servants are required.

On Saturday a charwoman came in to help make things ready for the new cook. She was a type of the charing sisterhood—big, red-faced, and noisy, with a tendency to order about the servants of the house. She scrubbed and scoured up everything in the basement, yet always stopped just short of finishing what she began. Every stewpan and pot received a rub and a dig with a knife, and was put back on the shelf with some of last year's grease or soot on it. To make things clean on the outside as well as on the inside seemed never to enter her head. The immense spit used for roasting was brought out, and by its looks I judged that the old cook had never troubled herself to wash it during the last six months. It was subjected to the process of scraping and pounding, which was enough to render it utterly useless ever after. It, too, was put back in the scullery, clean in spots.

That scullery! What a revelation it was to me, and how I resolved that when I got out I would use my influence to abolish sculleries for ever! I know that the majority of cooks insist upon having what they call a " place for doing the dirty work," but why should there be this dirty work, if things are done properly each day? To wash dishes and pots and kettles only hot water, plenty of soap and soda, and a dishcloth are necessary, and, if properly attended to after each meal, there is no reason why they should be put on the shelf with black soot sticking to them. I noticed that the charwoman and Annie seemed to have but one idea in their dish-washing—that of getting things put out of sight, no matter in what condition. When Annie brought the trays down from the dining-room, glasses, silver, knives, cups, meat-platters, and vegetable dishes were heaped together on the table in a miscellaneous mass, and, with the merest attempt at scraping and no effort to sort them, they were thrown into the water, which was immediately covered with a scum of grease and tea or coffee grounds. I took advantage of an opportunity to put my scientific method of dish-washing into practice, but failed to make any impression on Annie's mind, for she returned to her old way at supper-time. I first put all the glasses together, then emptied everything from cups and saucers, and placed them in a neat pile. Then the spoons, knives and forks, plates, meat and vegetable dishes, were cleansed of leavings and grease, and put in other piles near the dishpan, while all pots and kettles were cleaned out as thoroughly as possible with a knife, and hot water poured into them to soak off the remainder while I washed the best dishes.

These preliminary arrangements did not take more than five minutes, and then I was ready to proceed with dish-washing without the annoyance of greasy dish-water. The silver and glasses were washed and dried before I went on with the cups and plates, for I knew that, unless they were polished while they were hot, they would look smeared and dirty. I am aware that many servants insist on putting dishes away to dry on a rack, without applying a towel until they are ready to lay the table; but I have never seen a clean and well-polished dish that was so handled. If dish-racks were abolished along with the sculleries, mistresses would find less reason to complain of the tables being laid with smeared and nicked dishes. Nothing can be more aggravating and unsightly than an expensive set of china with cracks and bits chipped off the edges; and what little experience I had in the kitchen went to show me that all this could be prevented if dishes were washed, dried, and put away immediately after each meal.

Annie and I ate dinner on Saturday with the charwoman, who munched away at her bread and meat with her sleeves rolled up, exposing very fat, red arms. In the afternoon I was ordered to assist her in moving an iron bedstead from one room to another. She insisted that the bed could be pushed through the door without being taken apart, while I was of a different opinion. She did not look a pleasant person to cross, so I followed her instructions. The spirit was willing, but the flesh was weak, and, try as I would, I could not manage to lift the thing from the floor.

"Come on there, Liz! can't ye heft a bit?" she exclaimed impatiently. For the moment I forgot my

cap and apron, and remembered only my outraged
dignity and aching arms. Fortunately, ere I delivered
myself of a scathing rebuke for her familiarity, a
streamer flapped in my face, a timely reminder of my
altered condition and circumstances.

Thus the Allison family were spared the interesting scene of a combat between the housemaid and
the charwoman.

The bed finally had to be dismantled and taken
apart, and the charwoman seemed to regard me as
the cause of all the trouble. At tea-time she had
somewhat relented, and offered to share her pitcher of
bitter ale with me. (Mrs. Allison, I may mention,
showed the good sense not to supply the servants
with beer, and, if they drank it, it was at their own
expense.)

"Better take it, young woman," said she, as I
refused the glass she pushed towards me. "Ye'll
need a strengthener if yer housemaid in this place.
I've chared here five years, and I know the housemaid
they had before Annie came worked herself into the
'ospital in less than a year's time. She's done for
now, is Annie. Got housemaid's knee with all the
scrubbing."

I decided to investigate into the cause and cure of
this ailment, and took out a small note-book I carried
in my apron pocket, and wrote down a few shorthand
notes.

"What's them queer marks?" asked Annie, edging
around to my side of the table and looking over my
shoulder.

I explained that I was trying to learn stenography
with a view to bettering my position in life later on.

Annie smiled her approval of the project, and thought I should be able to earn as much as thirty shillings a week if I got a place.

The area gate bell rang just then, and Annie begged me to answer it, because I had finished tea and she had not. I started out, and got half-way up the stairs, when, looking up, I saw our own butcher's boy holding out a joint for me to take into the kitchen. " Hello, another new 'un!" he observed, and then, fearing he would recognise and betray me, I bolted backwards and into the kitchen, explaining that I had hurt my foot, and asked Annie to get the meat. From that time I lived in terror of being asked to go on hasty errands, when I would not have an opportunity to remove my cap and apron. It was not that I was ashamed of the badge, but simply that I did not care to be recognised in the guise by any friends or neighbours I might meet. I was always careful to wear my coat and hat when I posted the letters in the evening, much to the disgust of Annie, who insisted that I wasted too much time in " primping."

Saturday night the missing members of the family came home with their luggage and their maid. The boxes were heaped in the front hall and partly un-packed there. Mrs. Allison said that Annie and I were to carry them up-stairs the next morning, and I lay awake half the night wondering how I should be able to manage it without breaking any bones. Sunday morning we were allowed a half-hour's extra sleep ; but, to my astonishment, Annie informed me that the same round of work must be done as on weekdays. The stairs and passages, bedrooms, sitting-rooms, and drawing-rooms were to be swept and dusted, and I was busy until twelve o'clock as on former days. Then we had the various boxes to carry to the fourth floor. During the process Annie assured me that the weight seemed to be all at her end of the boxes, and I felt she had every reason to complain, though I tugged away with might and main. Women servants are not fitted for doing this sort of work, and in the case of families where no manservant is employed outside help should be brought in.

The gentleman of the house stood by, and saw us carrying the boxes and heard me remark that the cabman should have attended to them the previous night, but he seemed to be unimpressionable. Annie informed me that the evening before she had been obliged to assist the cabman in getting them from the top of the four-wheeler.

At two o'clock, as a meal for seven persons had to be cooked, Mrs. Allison asked me to wait at table while Annie stayed in the kitchen. I dressed in my very best for that auspicious occasion, for it was my *début* as a waitress. Annie gave me instructions beforehand, so that everything went off very creditably. Only once did I pass things to the right of the individual instead of to the left. No dishes were broken and nothing spilled over. I stood back in the corner of the dining-room awaiting orders from the head of the table, and many times had difficulty in repressing a smile as I listened to the table-talk. The first thought that occurred to me as I carried the heavy iron trays up the stairs was, "Why do not housewives spend a few pounds and have lifts put in, connecting dining-room and kitchen, thus saving all this running up and down stairs?" The trays were immense iron things that were in themselves very heavy without the addition of china and eatables. There are light tin trays to be had that answer every purpose, and I almost felt like suggesting the fact to Mrs. Allison after dinner, but I remembered her refusal of the whisk broom and desisted. It was half-past four when the dishes were cleared away. I began to feel anxious about my Sunday afternoon off, for I had received a letter, forwarded from the Camberwell address, telling me to call on Mrs. Brownlow, in Kensington, at six o'clock Sunday, as she thought she could employ me as parlourmaid. At five I asked permission to go out, which was granted. I found the Kensington lady a most charming person, and made arrangements to enter her service as parlourmaid the following Thursday evening, though how I should get rid of my present place I had not then decided. I was determined to try at least two situations before giving my experiences to the public, and I began to feel that my story of Mrs. Allison would not be a pleasant one to relate.

I returned at seven, and found Annie busily engaged in answering the door. It was Mrs. Allison's day at home. I helped to prepare the tea and cakes, later we served supper to the family, and at nine had our own bread and cheese. So this was a Sunday in service. I had two hours' rest; Annie had none! I remembered a command I had been taught in my youth which had to do with the keeping of the Sabbath, and said something about manservants and maidservants. I am not a Sabbatarian, but I contend that in the name of reason, and on good general business principles, every man and woman should have one day's rest during the week, be it Sunday or some other day. The round of sweeping should be omitted on Sunday, only a light dinner prepared, and a part of the servants be allowed to spend most of the day in their rooms, in church, or in the park, according to their inclinations, and the servants who must remain on duty during Sunday should be given a resting day during the week. I know it is asserted that most mistresses give their maids a whole or half-holiday each week, but my investigations have led me to believe that this is often neglected, and, whether or not it is so, the Sunday duties should be made as light as possible.

Monday evening the new cook made her appearance, and our board wages ceased. I did not do any marketing, thinking that henceforth we should be provided with suitable meals. For breakfast, Tuesday, bread and butter and coffee were placed on the table.

"Is there no meat or potatoes?" I questioned Annie.

"No, the missus never allows us anything in the morning but bread and coffee."

I was already tired with my morning's work, and, having been told I must "turn out" two rooms that day, I knew that, without a proper breakfast, I should not be able to get through. I would speak to Mrs. Allison about it.

"Better not," said Annie: "the last cook fried

some fish for breakfast one morning, and she got notice."

"Annie," I said, "I'm afraid this place is going to be too hard for me. I don't think I'll stop after my week is up."

"But you can't leave without giving notice. If you do, she'll make you pay her a whole month's wages ; and, if she makes you go without giving notice, she must pay you a month's wages," explained my co-worker.

"But suppose I do something she doesn't like and she discharges me ? "

"Why, then, you'd have to go ; but she wouldn't give you a character."

I went to Mrs. Allison's room and knocked at the door.

"Mrs. Allison, do you not allow the servants anything for breakfast but bread and coffee ? I thought there must be some mistake," I said, as she opened the door.

"No, it is not a mistake," was her reply.

"But I must have a good breakfast or I simply cannot do the work, so I will go out and buy some meat myself."

"Very well, do so," she answered as she shut the door.

An hour later, I was making her bed, when she entered the room.

"Lizzie, I have been thinking it over, and I have decided that you and I won't pull," was her announcement.

"No, I don't think we will, Ma'am," I replied.

"Then, if you will wait until I get suited," she continued, "you may go."

I told her I was sorry I could not accommodate her, but that I preferred to leave Thursday, and she went off in high dudgeon, saying that any common servant would show her mistress the courtesy to remain until she was suited.

Thus it came to pass that I was discharged from my first place without a character because I, like Oliver Twist, had the audacity to "ask for more." But I had three more days to work for Mrs. Allison, and I looked forward to Thursday with fear and trembling.

CHAPTER V.

WITHOUT A "CHARACTER."

When I informed Annie that I had been discharged, she exhibited the greatest concern, for to her mind my condition was a pathetic one. How should I get another place without the character Mrs. Allison would refuse to give? She argued that it was always better to part friends, even with bad mistresses, for without a character no girl could get a situation.

I made a note of this for future reference, and since I left service I have found it a useful bit of information. If many much-tried but good-natured mistresses would only remind impertinent and neglectful maids that future situations depend upon present good behaviour, a great stride would be made toward a solution of the servant problem. On the other hand, the time will come when references will be demanded from the mistress as well as the maid. Then the Mrs. Allison type will not be so numerous.

Poor Annie! She was holding one hand to her head and another at her side, while she discussed this question, displaying her unselfish interest in my welfare. She had lost four hours of legitimate sleep the preceding night, but was up at six in the morning as usual. What wonder that she felt tired and ill! I counselled her to go to bed and rest awhile. She looked at me again with the superior air she had worn on the evening of our first meeting. "When you're in service, you can't go to bed if you're ill," was her answer, as she carried the tray of silver and glasses into the pantry, and commenced her first day's work as *bonâ-fide* parlourmaid. She had only a servant-girl's headache, brought on by remaining awake till after one o'clock in order to open the door for the daughters of the house, who had been to the theatre! "But how avoid such occasional contingencies? Shall the young ladies be allowed a latchkey?" asks a horrified mother of grown-up daughters. Well, of course, to my unconventional mind, the latch-key would be the simplest way out of the difficulty; but I would suggest that it is the duty of the ladies' maid and not of the parlourmaid to wait up and serve supper after the theatre. The parlourmaid must rise early in the morning to begin her daily round of work, and therefore should be allowed to go to bed at a proper hour, while in the case of the ladies' maid it is, or should be, different. If she is up late, she should be allowed to sleep later in the morning. Of course, in large establishments of a dozen or more servants these matters are better arranged ; but in households like Mrs. Allison's, where the strictest economy is practised as regards the number of servants employed and the amount of wages paid, little or no attention is given to this important subject.

Mathilde, the Swiss maid, was a person who well appreciated her own value and took advantage of her position. She was a competent dressmaker and hair-dresser, who, for reasons known only to herself, elected to give her services to the Allison family for the small stipend of £20 a year. Realising that cheapness and competency rarely go together, Mrs. Allison knew that she would be unable to fill Mathilde's place at such a price, and decided it was best to humour that young woman's whims. Mathilde was of a sleepy nature, and could not be induced under any consideration to sit up after 10.30, so either Annie or I must remain down-stairs till all the family were in. It was Mathilde's duty to help me make the best beds, and while thus engaged I noticed that she had a patronising way of treating me. She was particularly inquisitive in regard to my previous life and occupation, and I told her a highly-entertaining story concerning myself.

The new cook was a welcome acquisition in the kitchen. Annie was especially glad to have some of the responsibilities taken off her shoulders, and the domestic machinery began to run a little more smoothly. My labours, however, were in no way lightened, except that I had nothing more to do with dish-washing.

Annie's duties were to rise at six o'clock, attend to the lamps, sweep and dust the large music-room, carry some boiling water to Mrs. Allison, lay the table, wait at all the meals, clear away and brush up afterwards, answer the door, and assist with the needlework. Her duties seemed neither so numerous nor so complex as my own, but when I explain that from half-past nine in the morning until eleven at night the bell rang on an average of every ten minutes it will be seen that her time was well occupied.

Mary, the cook, was tall, fat, ruddy-faced and good-humoured, and seemed inclined to make me her especial *protégé*. She expressed regret when I told her I was to leave the next Thursday, and gave me the address of a lady in Belgravia who she thought could offer me an easy place. At dinner she was greatly exercised over the news that neither beer nor beer-money was allowed in the kitchen, and blamed herself for her stupidity in forgetting to ask about so important a matter before she took the place. Beer, she declared, was essential to her health and happiness. Then she beamed upon me, and, handing me a pitcher, asked if I would run around the corner and get some bitter ale, as she could not leave the joint that was roasting before the fire. I did not wish to offend her, nor did I quite like the idea of going to a public-house ; but finally, as I stood there halting between two opinions, journalistic enterprise got the better of dignity. I threw on my hat and coat, and, with the despised pitcher in hand, made my exit from the area gate, determined to penetrate into the mysteries of the bar-room.

As I entered there came an odour of tobacco that nearly overwhelmed me, but I went forward to have my pitcher filled. There was over a score of men and women standing or sitting about on the long benches, drinking, smoking, and gossiping about what "she said," what "he said," and what "I said, sez I." Some of the men were in livery, and I was the only one of my sex without a cap and apron. A number of those present I recognised as servants in neighbouring families. They seemed in no hurry to return with their beer, and, judging by their hilarious state, many of them had been there some time, and various family secrets were divulged by one servant to another. I left the place with my pitcher of ale, which I tried to hide by means of a large morning paper and the cape of my coat. I had seen the result of allowing beer-money to servants, and I appreciated more keenly why so many of the letters I had received in answer to my advertisement had ended with the words "No beer." I found that the public-house was made a sort of rendezvous for the men and women servants of the neighbourhood, and housework lagged behind, while with pipe and beer they gossiped and dragged out family skeletons for the edification of their fellow-servants.

This question of beer-money is a much more serious one than many housewives imagine. I am speaking now from a purely business standpoint, for I am not a distributor of temperance tracts nor a member of a prohibition union. I can see no reason why beer or beer-money should be demanded by servants as one of their lawful rights. If, when their day's work is done, a glass of ale will help to take away "that tired

E

feeling" with which they must necessarily be afflicted, I would not be the one to deprive them of their comforter; but I do insist that the mistress of the house should not be called upon to furnish the beverage, nor should they under any circumstances be allowed to go to the public house to procure it. A business man in the city is not expected to furnish a daily allowance of beer to each one of his clerks; and, if domestic service is to be raised to a proper standard, this matter of beer-allowance must be dispensed with.

Mary was what is commonly called a plain cook —not a "professed" one, as she confidentially informed me; and when I noticed her way of preparing potatoes I decided that she was a very plain cook indeed. Her only ideas seemed to be either to boil them and send them up whole, or sift them through a colander, from which they emerged in dirty, rice-like flakes. She added no milk, butter, pepper, or salt, and I began to feel sorry for the family who were obliged to eat them—to say nothing of my own personal longing for some of the sixteen delicious dishes into which I knew potatoes could be made. Mary began at once to save up all the drippings from the roasts, and did not heed my remark that dripping was good for frying. She demanded to know whether I wanted to rob her of her lawful perquisites. When the bone-man came around, I believe she was richer to the extent of sixpence, while Mrs. Allison was poorer by a much larger amount.

I soon discovered that the cook had a prejudice against washing frying-pans, which, each time bacon or fish was cooked, were hung up in the scullery with the cold grease sticking to them, all in readiness for the next time they were needed; and it was only a matter of chance if the fish-pan was not used the next day for frying eggs. Another discovery I made was the reason why so many pieces of beautiful china soon get unsightly with the enamel all marked by an intricate network of dark cracks. It is done by putting the dishes into the oven or on the stove to heat before being taken up to the dining-room. This can be avoided by immersing the plates, meat-platters, and vegetable-dishes in very hot water and drying quickly just as they are ready to be sent up-stairs. The heat of the oven not only cracks them, but imparts a peculiar odour not likely to increase one's appetite at dinner.

After the cook came, the three beds in the servants' room were occupied, and, to my immense relief, Annie and Mary shared one washbowl, and left me in solitary enjoyment of the other. When we went to bed sleep did not come so easily as it had at first, for an exchange of opinions on various subjects was the order of the first hour or longer. Mary was curious to know all about the personal characteristics of each member of the family; but Annie was uncommunicative, and told her, if she stopped long enough, she would find out for herself. I was treated as a sort of heroine, Mary praising me for my pluck in asking for better breakfasts, which she declared her own intention of doing soon, and Annie always bewailing my characterless state. Mrs. Allison had advertised for a new housemaid, and Annie regaled us with an interesting description of all the girls who applied for the situation. At last a housemaid was engaged to come in the next Saturday.

E 2

"Why does she not come Thursday, so Mrs. Allison will have someone to take my place at once?" I asked.

"Oh, a girl don't like to go to a place as soon as she's engaged. A nice servant never does it," answered the cook.

"And why not, if it will accommodate the mistress?" I demanded.

"Well," said Mary, "I can't tell ye. I don't know as there's any pertickler reason, only they don't like it. Why, the missus wanted me to come a week ago, saying she was so put to without a cook; but I wouldn't do it. I don't approve of hurrying things like that."

By the dim candlelight I could see a self-satisfied smile on Mary's face, and I questioned her no more, concluding that servants, as well as other people, had a right to do things "on general principles" without assigning, or even having, any reason for their actions.

"I don't think I'll stay here after this year," remarked Annie, as she began to unbutton her boots.

"Why not?" I asked. "Don't you like it?"

"Of course I don't. Nobody could like such a hard place. But that isn't the reason. I've been here over a year now, and two years is long enough to stop in any place, good or bad. You get used to doing things the way to suit one missus, and, if you stay too long, it's hard to learn to suit other missuses, so I believe in changing round—that's my opinion."

Saying which, she threw her boots in the middle of the floor, and put her head under the pillow, instead of upon it. She always slept that way, and I

suspected that it was done to soften the clanging of
the alarm-bell which rang out fiercely at six every
morning. I did not always follow Annie in her line
of reasoning, and I could not quite understand her
objections to stopping a long time even in a good
place; but I put it down to the fact that she, like
the cook, acted sometimes " on general principles."

Annie, on the whole, was a good servant. She
took pride and interest in her work, and had at first
impressed me as being very conscientious. My faith
in this latter quality was a little shaken by an incident
that happened one day in the drawing-room. It was
before the cook came, and she was helping me to
wash some of the more expensive pieces of *bric-à-
brac*. I sat on the floor with a pail of water and a
cloth, cleaning some ivory and marble figures. I put
a small statue of Mercury into the pail, took it out,
and beheld that it was headless. I was bewildered,
for I had been particularly careful in the process, and
I knew I could not have knocked it against the pail.
As I sat with the head in one hand and the body in
the other, Annie startled me with, " The missus is
coming! Hide it quick, or she'll see it !"

" Of course, I shan't hide it," I retorted, angrily ;
and then Mrs. Allison came towards me.

" Oh, I forgot to tell you, Lizzie, that several of
these figures have been broken and glued together,
and ought not to be put in hot water. Lay it aside,
and I will mend it again."

Annie looked crestfallen and ashamed. Mrs.
Allison spoke pleasantly to me in those days. That
was before I had offended her by asking for better
breakfasts. Afterwards she sent me to " Coventry,"

and never looked at me except with forbidding brow.

Up to Wednesday I had escaped the scrubbing, for, when I turned out the young ladies' rooms the day before, I carefully arranged that twilight should come on before I got to that part of the work. Then the occupants were obliged to dress for dinner, and I would be in the way. Besides, the floor must not be damp when they went to bed, so they smilingly informed me that I need "never mind" about it. From that time I was their true friend, and when Miss Allison lay on the bed the next day with a jumping toothache I took my bottle of Pond's Extract to her and insisted that frequent applications would help her. In the evening, when she and Miss Blanche went to the theatre, I whistled for a hansom and helped them in with all the good grace imaginable, stepping up in front and closing the doors very carefully, so as not to catch their dresses. I even ceased to use "language" in my heart when pretty Miss Blanche, who had operatic aspirations, went from room to room screaming "a-a-ah" up and down through all the different keys. Both of them always wished me a cheery "Good-morning," even after I was discharged, and I have only the most pleasant recollections of them.

When, on Wednesday afternoon, the decree went forth that I should take up all the rugs in the drawing-room and scrub the floor, I felt that the evil day could no longer be put off, though how I was to carry through my commission was more than I knew. I dared not confide my ignorance to anyone, for when I engaged with Mrs. Allison, I assured her that

I had never been a servant, but had learned how to
work at home, which was true enough—at least, I
thought it was, for I knew the chapter headed
" Housemaids," in the book on " Servants' Duties," by
heart. But that chapter had said nothing about
scrubbing. I suppose the literary lady who wrote it
lived in a house where there was no scrubbing to be
done. Thus I was utterly in the dark as to how to
go at my task, and was obliged to follow my own
ideas on the subject. I took from my cupboard two
pails, one half full of soapy water, the other containing fresh water for rinsing, and with flannel and
brush I started out to do or die, or both. From the
conversation with the charwoman, I had gathered
that it was proper to go on one's knees for the operation ; but she had said that a former servant in this
family had got housemaid's knee by kneeling on the
cold floors. It was not part of my plan to contract
the disease, and then I was afraid of soiling and
wetting my print dress, which I wished to keep fresh
and neat-looking for my next place.

In scrubbing that drawing-room I kept two ideas
in mind : first, to ward off housemaid's knee ; second,
to keep myself and costume out of the wet. So
pinning up my frock, I took the brush and assumed a
squatting position, hopping about from place to place.
I scrubbed a square yard at a time, then rinsed in
clean water and dried it, congratulating myself the
while that I was something of a Columbus in my
way. I had nearly finished, when, glancing toward
the folding-doors, I saw Mrs. Allison looking at me,
her large black eyes burning with anger. Had I
been on the ground-floor, I am sure I should have

jumped from the window and precipitately departed from my situation, so dangerous did the lady of the house appear.

"Well, a pretty servant you make, I must say! Any girl with half a grain of sense would know how

MY SYSTEM OF SCRUBBING.

to scrub. You haven't even got general intelligence!" was the announcement that burst from her. Now I had always been told that I had a large bump of combativeness and was able to hold my own in a dispute; but this time I was speechless, feeling that my position really was untenable. I had nothing to say in my own defence; but a sense of the ridiculous overcame my prudence, and I smiled blandly in Mrs.

Allison's face. She uttered a contemptuous, impatient "Oh!" and left me.

I hurriedly finished the room, put the rugs and furniture in place, and, perched on the top of the step-ladder, polished the looking-glasses with tissue-paper. The steps were more than twice my own height, and when I attempted to lift them from one part of the room to another I found it a case of "when Greek meets Greek," and was obliged to pull them along after me as best I could.

That evening Annie again broached the needle-work subject, fearing, I suppose, that I would go on the morrow and leave her to clear out the mending-basket. I had postponed it as long as I well could, without admitting point-blank that I was unable to cope with the task, so I determined to do unto Annie as I would have her do to me under similar circumstances. I remembered to have seen my mother put a wooden ball into the toes and heels when she darned stockings, and I asked Annie for the darning-ball. She had never heard of such a thing.

"But I must have one, or I can't darn them," I insisted.

She brought me an oval-shaped soda-water bottle.

"Maybe that'll do. It's sort of round," she said.

I thought it would, and, feeling that "well begun is half done," I attacked the enemy, and darned to the best of my ability. If the wearers of those stockings got bad feet on account of the lumps and seams, I can only say I am very sorry, and pledge my word to avoid mending-baskets hereafter.

On Thursday I washed out all the dusters and made my cupboard as tidy as possible preparatory

to taking my departure.   Mrs. Allison did not speak
to me again after the scrubbing episode.   When at
six o'clock I informed her that I was ready to go,
she silently handed me six shillings, which was really
liberal, for she only owed me five shillings and fourpence halfpenny.   I thanked her and said good-bye,
but she did not answer.   I do not doubt that long
before this she has realised the bad taste she displayed in thus showing her temper.

In my story of my life at Mrs. Allison's house
I have spoken of her only as a mistress.   Some of
my friends who know her personally have assured
me that, socially and intellectually, she is a most
charming woman to meet.   I did not go into
her house as an enemy or detective to pry into her
private affairs.   Although many opportunities were
given me for doing this, I refused to take advantage
of them.   I was a journalist seeking information on
a certain subject.   She happened to answer my
advertisement, and was the first person who offered
me a place, which I accepted.   I have given an
account of my experiences at her house as a servant ;
that is all.   Mr. Allison, who is a man well known
in the professional world, was always pleasant with
me ; Mr. John Allison, the eldest son, treated me
politely, but always with dignity ; while the nice
ways of Master Tom won my admiration from the
first.   Miss Kate, the youngest member of the family,
went to the country shortly after I arrived, and I
saw little of her.

When I left Mrs. Allison's house I went to a
jeweller's and left the six shillings she paid me to
be made into a bracelet.   Then I jumped into a cab

and was driven to Mrs. Brownlow's in Kensington, where I was to enter another situation ; this time as parlourmaid.

CHAPTER VI.

PARLOURMAID TO MRS. BROWNLOW.

MRS. BROWNLOW'S residence was a pretty little house in Kensington, with the name "Elsmore Lodge" done in gold letters over the highly-polished dark green door. The brass bells, knocker, and letter-box shone out like new mirrors, and, as I stood waiting for my ring to be answered, I could see my reflection in the door-plate. The great wide hall into which I was admitted by the housemaid seemed to have been newly carpeted for the winter, and bright-coloured rugs were strewn about the floor. The housemaid, who informed me that her name was Alice, told me that Mrs. Brownlow had gone out to dinner, and had instructed her to show me to my room. I had already, on the preceding Sunday, been shown through the house by Mrs. Brownlow, who said that, of course, I must see the house before I could tell whether I would like the situation ; but Alice thought I had better take another look over the place, and to humour her I followed her from one room to another.

On either side of the front hall there was a large room, one the dining-room, the other the library. The dining-room was covered with Japanese matting, with a large crumb-cloth in the centre, and other rugs scattered about. The furniture was of beautiful old English oak and leather, and many pictures of game, fruit, fish, horses, and dogs hung on the wall. In a corner Alice called my attention to a lift, connecting the kitchen and dining-room. She explained that, before laying the table, I was to put all the china on the lift and draw it up, and that the cook would send up the meats and vegetables just as the family sat down.

"You'll have to toe the mark if you keep this place," said she confidentially. "Missus sent the last parlourmaid away because she didn't make the glasses shine and broke so many dishes. Just before she left she broke a big punch-bowl and a lot of cups, and never told. Missus found it out a few hours before she went, and took out a part of her wages for it. It was a shame, wasn't it?"

"Why, no, I don't think so. What right had she to break the dishes and not say anything about it? And, besides, if it was her fault, she ought to pay for them," I answered, for the moment putting myself in Mrs. Brownlow's place and feeling that I should have done the same thing under similar circumstances.

A very unpleasant look gathered on Alice's face as I said it.

"Oh! so you take the part of the missus against the servants, do you? I don't."

From that time I knew I had an enemy.

We went into the library, which was decorated in Oriental style. There were pictures, books, newspapers, magazines, two writing-desks, and a large music-box in a corner, which, after Alice had set it in motion, played me a merry welcome to my new situation. Up the wide staircase, padded and carpeted so that no footfalls could be heard, we went to the drawing-room on the first floor. The room was not so elegant nor so large as that at Mrs. Allison's, but it was pretty and homelike, with the appearance of having been furnished more for comfort than display. Mrs. Brownlow's bedroom came next—a veritable bower of pink. The dressing-table, I noticed, was at the side of the window, and not in front, as is the usual custom. Adjoining this room was the sewing-room, which, Alice said, would also be used by the maid as a sleeping-room, as Mrs. Brownlow had made some changes in order to give me a bedroom to myself. On the next floor was the bath-room in which was a gas geyser, a bedroom for Miss Brownlow, the daughter of the house, Mr. James Brownlow's room, and two servants' rooms. The room occupied by Alice and the cook was a large, comfortable place with red ingrain carpet on the floor. There were two toilet-tables and bureaus combined, with separate washbowls, soap-cups, &c., bright pictures on the walls, and no religious mottoes. Then I went into my own room, a snug little place which Mrs. Brownlow had just fitted up for me. It was very cosy, had fresh carpet, and a nice clean set of single bedroom furniture. The little bed had a good mattress and springs, and was covered with a spotless white quilt. Under the mantel there was a small gas-grate. Alice told me there were no coal-fires in the house, and that even the cooking was done by gas. Each room had a gas-stove in the grate, and it was only required to strike a match to light the fires. She added, however, that, for some reason, Mr. Brownlow did not quite like the gas-fires, and was negotiating with a stove company to build and put up a large furnace in the cellar, and thus heat all the halls and rooms by registers, after the American plan. On my first interview Mrs. Brown-low had told me that the servants were allowed to have fires in their rooms in the morning and evening, and when changing their dresses in the afternoon, provided they were always careful to turn off the gas when they went to bed or left the room.

As I put away the few clothes I had brought with me, Alice stood waiting for me.

"Where's your box?" she asked, noticing my very small handbag.

"It is at my lodgings in Camberwell. I thought I wouldn't go to the expense of bringing it here till I knew whether I would suit Mrs. Brownlow. I've never been in service before, you know," was my answer.

In the basement, Alice took me about and showed me the various china cupboards, and the pantry where I was to wash the glass and silver. As none of the family were at home to dinner, I had no waiting at the table. At eight o'clock we had our own dinner, which consisted of a joint, potatoes, brussels sprouts, and a boiled pudding. There were four of us—Sarah the cook, Janette the French maid, Alice, and myself. We had plenty of dinner, which was well-cooked and nicely-served, and I learned that usually the family and the servants had the same food. The table was spread in a comfortable little room off the kitchen, and the knives, forks, and spoons were not of the peculiar brassy variety supplied to the servants at Mrs. Allison's. Sitting opposite to Alice, I had a good opportunity to study her. She was tall, with a pretty face and trim figure, but she had the appearance of being treacherous and dishonest, and I wondered how she had managed to remain in her situation so long. Janette I liked very much better, and the cook seemed a pleasant, good-natured sort of woman. After dinner Alice went up-stairs to tidy the rooms, and I remained in the kitchen until about half-past nine. I watched the cook wash up the dishes, and saw that she did the work after the manner of Annie and the cook at Mrs. Allison's. The cooking utensils were not washed at all, but put up on the scullery table to remain until the next morning. The dishes rattled together in the pan, and chip after chip came off through her careless manner of handling them.

When Mrs. Brownlow returned, I was asked to go to her room. She was particularly kind in her manner of treating me, not in a patronising way, but as one woman talking to another who was less fortunate than herself. Although she evinced more interest in my previous history than had Mrs. Allison, she asked all her questions with tactful delicacy. She said she was anxious that I should think of her as much in the light of a friend as a mistress, although she paid me money for the work I was to do, and expected it to be well done. She explained that in employing me she was making an experiment, and, if she found it a successful one, she would make an entire change in her staff of servants, and engage girls of education to take the places of the cook and housemaid.

"I have given you a bedroom alone," said Mrs. Brownlow, "because I thought you would find it much pleasanter to keep to yourself. You will probably want it quiet for reading and writing in the evening and on Sunday."

I fully appreciated Mrs. Brownlow's thoughtfulness in regard to the bedroom, although I could not help regretting that, under the circumstances, I would not be able to hear the night gossip of the cook and housemaid. Before leaving I was given the following list of the parlourmaid's duties :—

"Rise at seven o'clock, and be ready for the servants' breakfast at 7.15. Afterwards sweep and dust the front hall and drawing-room, lay the table for the nine o'clock breakfast, wait at table and clear away, attend to the glass and silver, light gas-fires in drawing- and dining-rooms, sweep and dust the dining-room, clean the lamps, lay the table for one o'clock luncheon, clear away, prepare for dinner and wait at table. After each meal shake the crumb-cloth, and answer the door during the day. Always to be dressed in time for luncheon."

Besides this daily round, a part of each day in the week was to be given to some special work, such as turning out the drawing-room, dining-room, cleaning silver, &c. On Saturday I was to assist the housemaid in airing and repairing the table and bed linen, the needlework of the family being done by the ladies' maid. I was to have an afternoon off each week, and be allowed to go to morning or evening service on Sunday, if I desired. On Sunday it was arranged that each servant should have half the day to herself, and the cook had every Sunday afternoon off, a mid-day dinner being served, and either Alice or I preparing and clearing away the eight o'clock supper.

Mrs. Brownlow's list did not terrify me as Mrs. Allison's had done, for the amount of work required was not unreasonable, and there was no starting with the day's work without breakfast. Mrs. Brownlow told me she had experienced considerable trouble in regard to the cleaning of knives, blacking of boots, and scrubbing the front step, each servant declaring it was the other's place to do these things, until finally she had procured the services of a member of the Houseboy's Brigade, who came every morning to do this work, while once a week a larger boy from the same place washed all the windows in the house. It seemed to me most disgraceful that there should have been rioting in the kitchen over a few knives and boots. With such a small family and convenient house, three servants should have done the work easily. I told Mrs. Brownlow that I was perfectly willing to clean the knives and the boots, but she only smiled and said—

"We will wait a few weeks and see how things turn out."

That night, comfortable as my bed was, I did not soon go to sleep, for Mrs. Brownlow's kind face and gentle manners were always in my mind, and I began to think over a plan by which I might supply her with a good servant when I left, provided, of course, everything should prove satisfactory on both sides.

At 7.15 the next morning we sat down to the kitchen breakfast, which consisted of fried bacon,

F

potatoes, toast, and coffee. I complimented Sarah on her tasty way of cooking, and she smiled benignly, saying that she had been a professed cook for ten years, and hoped she did know something about her business. William Johnson, the brigade boy, came in about 7.30, and the cook, remarking that she supposed he was as hungry as usual, put a large plate of bread-and-butter and a cup of coffee before him with the knives and boots. I had seen hungry boys before, but I really never came in contact with a growing boy who had such a capacity for bread and coffee as William Johnson. In six minutes he had disposed of five large thick slices of bread and three cups of coffee.

" Don't you have any breakfast before you go to work ? " I asked.

"Yes'um, at half-past five, but I gets hungry again," was his reply.

In half an hour I was ready to sweep the drawing-room, while Alice started to clean the stairs and landings.

" The other parlourmaid always swept the front hall first, and I think it's the best way," she observed as I opened the drawing-room door, with broom and dustpan in hand.

" I should say that was a very bad way," I answered. "What is the use of my sweeping the front hall while you sweep the stairs and landings above ? Some of the dust would drop down, and you would dirty it as fast as I cleaned it. You sweep while I attend to the drawing-room, and I'll do the hall afterwards."

She looked very snappish, and declared she did

not approve of new-fangled notions, and what was the difference anyhow, so long as I could say I had done it ?

In laying the breakfast-table I found that all the glasses were smeared and covered with finger-marks, while the silver looked as if it had never been properly washed. There was egg or paste, or something of the kind, between the prongs of every fork. I was aware that in many instances parlourmaids overcame these difficulties by using their aprons as towels ; but, not quite approving of that plan, I sent the things down on the lift and washed them again. After breakfast, looking on my list, I saw that Friday was the day for cleaning the silver. Mrs. Brownlow informed me that Clara, my predecessor, had always left the powder in the crevices of the plate, declaring she could not remove it, however much she brushed, and added, " I hope you will find a way of getting it off." After rubbing it I washed and brushed it in hot water with soap and ammonia, which removed every particle of white dust. Mrs. Brownlow was so pleased with the result that she avowed her intention of making me her deputy-housekeeper.

" You see," said she, " I am so interested in my painting and music that I do not like to keep my mind too much on household matters, but I do want everything clean and nice."

I did not tell her how fully I appreciated her situation, nor of my unfitness for the position of housekeeper.

When I attended to the lamps, they looked as if they had not been well trimmed and cleaned for the past few months. The wicks were crooked and

F 2

crusted, while the ventilating burners were completely filled up with lampblack and dirt. After vainly trying to remove it with a pin and brush, it occurred to me that the only possible way to get rid of it would be to boil all the burners. So I put them in a saucepan on the stove, with plenty of hot water and soda, and in an hour they came out bright and clean. As I was putting the chimneys in a basin preparatory to washing them, Alice made some excuse to come into the pantry, and said she never had seen such goings on as stewing lamp-burners and putting chimneys in water, which was sure to break them. They should be cleaned with a cloth and chimney-brush. As I paid no attention to her, she soon left me, and expressed her opinion to the cook of "them smart girls that knows so much." At dinner I had the satisfaction of overhearing Mr. Brownlow remark to his wife, "That girl's a jewel! See the chimney how it shines, and not a particle of odour about the lamp!"

It was with considerable consternation that I attempted to open the first bottle of wine at the dinner-table. I had practised parlourmaiding to some extent before I left home, and had proudly acquired the knack of folding serviettes in the shape of a slipper, but try as I would I had found myself unable to manage a corkscrew. Had I been permitted to go into the hall with the bottle, I think I might have accomplished the feat a little more satisfactorily. The cork broke off, and at last I was obliged to push the remainder of it into the bottle, and a part of the contents came whizzing up in my face. After that accident it seemed to me everything went wrong, and I several times had to stop and ponder over which was my right hand and which my left, and put myself exactly behind the person I was serving before I ventured to put down a plate or a knife and fork. I could have wept for joy when I heard Mr. James Brownlow remark, " Mother, I don't

"THE CONTENTS CAME WHIZZING UP IN MY FACE."

mind opening the wine hereafter. I think it is rather hard work for a girl."

The next day, after I had opened the door for a visitor, Mr. Brownlow met me in the hall, and said, " Lizzie, do you know the difference between a friend of the family and a bill-collector ? "

" Yes, sir, I think I do," I replied, remembering that in my own experience I had often found a very painful difference between the two.

" Well, now, you must not let any collectors get into this house for the next month. I'm in Paris, see ? Don't wait till they tell you what they want, but you must be able to spot them on sight, and say at once I'm not in London. That last girl of ours got me in more trouble by her stupidity in letting tax-gatherers and dressmakers and tailors in the house. Said she didn't know how she was going to tell what they wanted when they wouldn't give their business. To be a good parlourmaid you must be a mind-reader, and you look as if you could do something in that line."

I bowed my acknowledgment of the compliment, and promised to do my best. I knew that in order to fulfil my part of the compact I must bring to play all my native powers of discernment. If I had had small tradespeople to deal with, my task would have been an easy one ; or, if all bill-collectors had been accommodating enough to wear pot-hats, I might still have experienced no difficulty. Mrs. Brownlow had told me, when she engaged me, that, after the first month, she would increase my wages, and had let drop a hint that her husband, a stockbroker in the City, was at present a little short of money because of the hard times in America, where he was largely interested in certain securities ; so I had no difficulty in understanding Mr. Brownlow's objection to a particular class of visitors.

Half an hour after my conversation with the head of the house the bell rang, and I opened the door to a tall, handsome-looking man, having all the appear-ance of belonging to the gentry. It was only about 10.30, and I could not believe the man had come to make a party call at that time in the morning, so when he asked for Mr. Brownlow I said, "He's gone to Paris; but will you please tell me your business?"

"Oh, no, it's not necessary; I'll see Mrs. Brownlow. She will do quite as well."

Now, I had been warned against men who would not tell their business, and I said, "She's gone to Paris, too, and won't be back for a month."

"Well, it's a fine performance; that's all I've got to say," was his answer, as he turned to go.

"Won't you leave your name?" I asked.

"No," he replied, rather savagely, and walked out.

I congratulated myself on my prowess, and went up-stairs to describe the man to Mrs. Brownlow, when I discovered that I had turned away the wrong man. Still, I was not disheartened by my first failure, and after two or three days' practice I became quite an expert in that line. The experience I thus gained was not only of immense service to Mr. Brownlow, but will probably prove of great value to me personally.

In a few days I had become quite accustomed to my duties, and I felt that the position of parlour-maid at Elsmore Lodge was not a hard one. Mrs. Brownlow was one of the most considerate women I had ever met, and tried in every way to make her servants comfortable; but neither the cook nor Alice showed any appreciation of her kindness. Both of them were continually on the defensive, and seemed to believe that mistress and servant must necessarily look upon each other as enemies. Sarah cooked well, but her extravagance was appalling. In spite of Mrs. Brownlow's order that all the small pieces of bread should be used up for puddings and dressing, Sarah allowed them to remain in the bread-box until they moulded, and then threw them away; while sugar, potatoes, and cold meat disappeared with the most astonishing rapidity. Alice aided and abetted her in every possible way. I began to wonder if, after all, good treatment was appreciated by many of the girls who went out to service, and I decided that it did not always follow that a kind mistress made a good servant.

CHAPTER VII.

MY LAST DAYS IN SERVICE.

DURING my stay at Mrs. Brownlow's I discovered that domestic labour, arranged in a reasonable manner, was not in itself difficult work. Not having a taste for household duties, and having had no experience except that gained by practising some of the parlour-maid's duties at home and a week's observation and work at Mrs. Allison's, I was not, of course, so well equipped as a well-trained domestic servant would have been; but, in spite of these drawbacks, I did the work quickly and neatly, and Mrs. Brownlow informed me that none of her former servants had suited her so well. She began at once to plan how she might dispense with ordinary domestics, and replace them by young women who would take a genuine interest in their work and render her something more than eye service. Sarah was an excellent cook, and there was no fault to be found with the food as it was prepared for the table ; but she was afflicted with a very common complaint among cooks, laziness, and was continually talking about the need of a kitchen-maid, although the whole basement was conveniently fitted up, and the cook's duties were so light that her mistress did not feel disposed to hire an assistant for her. Mrs. Brownlow had consented, at the cook's request, to have only one set of meals prepared, except as regarded the servants' breakfast, the kitchen breakfast coming earlier, as a matter of course. At eleven they were allowed a light luncheon, and at half-past one, after the family had lunched, the servants ate the same food as was served at the dining-room table, and for the night dinner it was arranged that they could dine immediately after dessert was served. Although these changes in the usual routine of servants' meals were made to please the cook and lighten her labours, she did not show any appreciation of the favour, and positively refused to scrub the doorstep, clean the knives, or black the boots, which she declared was not " her place," while the housemaid insisted that she did not " bargain for that business."

Mrs. Brownlow was a woman of gentle, even temper, who took for her motto, " Live peaceably with all men, if it be possible," and so to preserve anything like the semblance of order in her household, she hired the brigade boy to attend to these things, and was constantly putting herself to trouble and expense for the sake of her servants. She had a decided talent for artistic work, and was interested in music, and, as she explained to me, she did not care to devote her whole attention to the management of her house. Her daughter, a young lady of about twenty, had but recently made her *début* in society, and had literary aspirations, as she one day confided to me. She did not wish to turn housekeeper, and the French maid did not understand enough English to act as deputy for her mistress. If the servants had been of the sort who would perform their duties conscientiously, Mrs. Brownlow need have devoted only one hour each morning to overlooking the housekeeping ; but, as it was, they took advantage of her kind and easy way, and the two chief qualities displayed by the cook and housemaid were indolence and extravagance.

"Why do you not wipe the hot-water cans before you set them in the hall ?" I said one morning to Alice, who had been distributing the water at the different bedroom doors.

"Because it's too much trouble," she answered, with a toss of her head.

"But you will ruin the carpet," I insisted.

"Well, it's not your carpet, so you will please mind your own business," she retorted.

Now, what could be done with a girl so perfectly devoid of honour ? I asked her how she expected to keep a situation, and how she could get a character, if she did not try to please her mistress.

"Well, I'd make a time if she wouldn't give me a character," was her answer, as she went to the next floor dripping water over the stairs.

And she did "make a time ;" for the very next day Mrs. Brownlow, losing all patience with her because she would not turn the mattresses or even take the quilts entirely off before making the beds, said, "Alice, I cannot put up with your careless habits any longer, and I wish you would look for a new situation. I give you notice to-day."

Alice replied, " I'll go to-day if you'll give me a month's wages and let me have a character."

"It will be impossible for me to give you a character, unless it is a very bad one," answered her mistress.

And then the "time" commenced. Alice threatened her with all the dreadful consequences imaginable; said she knew certain things she would tell all over London, and accused Mrs. Brownlow of taking the bread out of her mouth. She did not become quiet until Mr. James Brownlow came in and gave her what he described as a "dressing down," when she slunk away to the kitchen, whimpering about the cruelties of mistresses, and giving her opinion in no gentle terms of certain kinds of parlourmaids.

However, she did not leave that day, probably deciding that it would be better to remain her month out, with the hope that she might, after all, obtain the "character" to help her secure another situation. On Sunday she took her half-day off, going out immediately after breakfast, and I did the bedroom work that morning. Everything was much more convenient and comfortable than it had been at Mrs. Allison's. Two of the rooms being on the same floor with the bathroom, the filling of the water-pitchers was an easy matter, and I had only to go down one flight of stairs to carry water to Mrs. Brownlow's room. With the assistance of Janette, I was through all the work by eleven o'clock, and was able to rest until it was time to lay the table for the two o'clock dinner. In the afternoon I remained in my room, attending to some newspaper correspondence, and writing a long letter to the Editor of the *Weekly Sun*. I requested him to look up for me a superior young woman, thoroughly domesticated, who would be willing to take a situation as parlourmaid in Mrs. Brownlow's house when I left the following Thursday, as he knew I must do. I gave a full description of the family, the house, and a list of the duties expected of the parlourmaid. Then I made arrangements to have a telegram sent me on Wednesday requesting my presence in the City that afternoon on important business, which would appear to give me a plausible excuse for resigning my situation.

That night I slept the sleep of the just, and awoke Monday morning feeling fortified against all the attacks of Alice, my enemy. We were engaged all day in preparing for Mrs. Brownlow's reception, which was to be given in the evening. Two extra servants were hired to answer the door and assist in waiting on the guests, who began to arrive about half-past nine. At twelve o'clock I was serving punch and sweets in the drawing-room, and was getting on famously, when I heard someone exclaim under his breath, "Well, my eyes!" and, looking towards the speaker, I recognised an acquaintance, a well-known London publisher. In spite of my consternation, I was rather amused at the look of bewilderment on his face; for he knew nothing of the experiment I was making, and two weeks before I had entertained him in my own home. My cap and apron had not disguised me as much as I had hoped, and, knowing the proclivity of the male sex to gossip, I began to pull my wits together to plan a way to prevent a catastrophe and save myself from detection. When I went to the dining-room for further supplies, I hurriedly wrote on a slip of paper, "You don't know me, understand," and, returning to the drawing-room, I slipped the note into his hand as I passed him a plate of sandwiches. Then he was seized with sudden convulsions of laughter, which nearly made me lose my equilibrium, but I felt sure that he was a true friend and would not tell when he understood my position. Later I opened the door for him, and as he passed me he whispered, " What's it for?" and I answered, " A book for you to publish," whereupon he left the house and jumped into a hansom, humming " Oh, my Mary Ann."

I seemed to be fated to have romantic adventures at Elsmore Lodge. Tuesday night I went to bed at the usual time, 10.30, and I thought I had only slept a few minutes when I was awakened by the ding-a-ling of the front-door bell. Lighting a match, I discovered that it was three o'clock. The house was perfectly quiet except for the bell, which seemed to be summoning me down-stairs unto dreadful things I knew not of. To say that I was afraid to go to the door only mildly expresses my feelings. My room was a back one, so I could not first look out of the window and inspect the bearing of the visitor. Finally I plucked up a small amount of courage, donned my dress and slippers, and with a night-lamp I started down-stairs, trying to shame myself into bravery. Was I not a journalist? Ha I not bearded many a lion in his den, and should now tremble at being obliged to go to the door at three o'clock in the morning?   It was of no use; the further down-stairs I got, the more my knees knocked together from very fear, and I had to admit to myself that I was nothing but a very timid woman, after all.   Then I thought of a way by which I could view the ringer of the bell at a distance before opening the door, and I went into the library, noiselessly

"THERE ON THE STEP STOOD MR. JAMES BROWNLOW."

unbolted and drew up the window, and looked out. There on the step stood Mr. James Brownlow, ringing the bell with one hand and with the other vainly trying to insert the key in the lock. I took in the situation at once. He had been at the Savage Club. I quietly closed the window again and opened the door, uttering not a word and trying my best to look respectful and sedate. "Thank you. Don't mention it to anybody," he said, passing up-stairs, while I fastened and bolted the door. So there I was, with a secret on my soul, and not allowed to tell it to anybody! How I should have enjoyed repeating the story to one of his brother Savages; but that was impossible, so I had to content myself to keep it until I got out of service, knowing that then I could unburden myself to the public.

I became quite an expert in laying and waiting on the table, and I grew proud of my skill in making it look beautiful with bright china and silver. When I took off the table-cloth I was always careful to fold it in the same creases. I used a brush in cleaning out the crevices of the cut-glass tumblers and dishes. I made such an improvement in their appearance that they elicited the admiration of all the family, especially of Mr. James Brownlow, who took frequent occasion to compliment me on the improved condition of things in general, and even went so far as to say that he thought the most sensible employment for all poor girls was domestic service, for which work I seemed particularly fitted. I did not feel at liberty to argue the point with him at that time, nor did I attempt to disabuse his mind of his very pleasant impression. I only thought that if I, in the face of so many difficulties, was able to satisfactorily perform the duties of a parlourmaid, what could not a girl with inclination and training do?

Miss Mary Brownlow took quite a fancy to me, and one day broached the subject of my being her personal attendant and companion—a sort of private secretary for her while she was engaged in writing

various newspaper and magazine articles, which, so
far as I could determine, were generally returned to
her in the stamped envelope she enclosed. I told
her it was impossible for me to hold such a position,
that my handwriting was neither beautiful nor easily
read. Then she suggested that I should learn typewriting and take dictation from her, while I was
obliged to use all my self-control to keep back a
smile, wondering what her astonishment would be
if she could see me a week later writing up my
experiences at her home on my own beloved
typewriting machine.

" Oh, I could never learn, I am sure, and I would
not like to be a secretary. I'd rather be a parlourmaid," I said.

In the kitchen everything went at sixes and
sevens. Alice, although less impertinent in her treatment of her mistress, vented her spite on me, and
tried to the best of her ability to drive me mad with
her constant insinuations that I was to blame for her
discharge, and threatened to pay me up for it some
day. She said she had lost two of her handkerchiefs
the day before, and vaguely hinted that I used some
just like them, till, what with the loud talking,
bickering, and general uproar, I feared my head
would completely give way. As it was, I was seized
with a violent headache, which Mrs. Brownlow observed, and sent me up-stairs to lie down, while Miss
Mary Brownlow—dear heart!—tried to doctor me
with the laying on of hands and brown paper satu-
rated in vinegar. It was her own remedy, and she
recommended it very highly. It really did me good,
and at luncheon I was up and about again. A

few hours later, when we were having our tea, the door-bell rang, and I jumped up to answer it.

"Go out in the area, and see who it is before you go up. Maybe it's only a tramp," said the cook.

"But perhaps it's one of Mrs. Brownlow's friends, and suppose she looked down into the area and saw me. Do you think that would appear nice?"

"Well, do as you like. I only tried to save you steps," was her ungracious reply.

This going to the area to view a visitor from a distance is a very common practice among parlour-maids and menservants. I have often noticed it at houses where I have called. There cannot possibly be any excuse for it in a well-ordered house, yet I have seen it among servants of the very best people. I was discouraged with trying to instil right principles of action into Alice's and Sarah's minds. It was sowing seed on stony ground. The motto which they seemed to think was the proper one between kitchen and drawing-room was "War to the knife." The morning after the entertainment Alice chipped off a piece of a very handsome and expensive cut-glass dish, and said nothing to Mrs. Brownlow about it, although I begged her to do so. It placed me in rather an awkward position, for I did not wish to gain the reputation of being a tale-bearer, nor did I think it right for Mrs. Brownlow to remain in ignorance of the affair. In the afternoon she came down to the pantry to show me about rearranging the glass and china cupboards, and noticed the broken dish at once. She knew that she had sent Alice down-stairs with it, and, of course, concluded she had broken it; but when Alice was questioned she stoutly denied it,

G

saying it was whole when she put it in the cupboard.
But her mistress had occasion to remember other
incidents, and, although she refrained from openly
accusing Alice, I could see that she knew who was
the culprit.

The cook was a very intelligent sort of person,
well versed in her profession, and, had she cared to do
so, she might have made a valuable servant. When
she felt so inclined, she was able to manufacture the
most delicious little side-dishes from small bits of
meat, fish, or other things left over, though she
oftener chose to present such things to her sister, who
was almost a daily visitor in the kitchen. Sarah gave
me occasional hints in regard to certain household
work. She showed me how to clean the water carafes
by the use of shot, how to restore gilt frames by
rubbing them with turpentine, and she also informed
me that I could keep the silver bright for a long time
by placing a lump of camphor in the silver chest. I
noticed that she always kept an oyster shell in the
tea-kettle, which, she explained, collected all the sedi-
ment that usually gathers in such kettles and often
makes the water look muddy. If she had only done
as well as she knew, she would have indeed proved to
be " a treasure."

Wednesday, a telegram addressed to " Elizabeth
Barrows " came to Elsmore Lodge. It was from my
solicitor, and read, " Come to my office at once.
Important news concerning your father's relatives.
Must go to Liverpool." Thinking to prepare Mrs.
Brownlow for my resignation, I showed her the
message.

" Perhaps it is good news for you. How nice that

would be! though I would not like to have you leave me," she said, and then told me I might go to the City at once.

I went to the office of the *Weekly Sun.* There I met a sensible young woman, named Lucy Atkins, the daughter of a physician with whom one of the members of the staff had been acquainted. She was refined and quiet, but tall and strong in appearance, and she assured me that she was particularly well versed in all matters connected with domestic work. I promised to use my influence to get the situation for her. I returned to Mrs. Brownlow, and told her I had received news which necessitated my presence in Liverpool, and that I was likely to come into the possession of a small yearly income, which would do away with the necessity of my remaining in service. Had it been possible, I should have preferred to tell the whole truth to Mrs. Brownlow; but I knew that could not be done for the present, and I was obliged to invent an excuse for leaving her. Then I told her that, appreciating her kind treatment, and knowing what a comfortable situation a girl might find with her, I had endeavoured to get her another servant in my place—not a servant of the ordinary kind, but a woman of intelligence, thoroughly domesticated, and able to perform the duties much better than I had done. Mrs. Brownlow was kindness itself, and the whole matter was quickly arranged. I telegraphed for Lucy Atkins to call, and she came that evening for an interview. The next morning she brought her box and entered upon the situation, and I spent the day in showing her what I knew of the work. It happened that she

G 2

had two friends, a widow and her daughter, who wished a place together, the mother as cook-house-keeper and the daughter as housemaid or parlour-maid, and Mrs. Brownlow wrote, asking them to call on her with the object of taking them into her service if she was suited. When I was ready to leave, Mrs. Brownlow offered me my week's wages, which I refused to take, asking her to give the money to some other girl who would need it more than I. When I said good-bye, she told me to call on her as soon as possible and tell her all about myself and how I was getting on. I said that I would do so, and I fully intended to keep my promise, and explain the whole matter to her in the near future.

CHAPTER VIII.

THE MERITS OF DOMESTIC SERVICE.

WHEN I left Mrs. Brownlow's I went at once to Camberwell to give up the lodgings I had been supposed to occupy, and to instruct the lodging-house keeper as to what course she was to pursue in case further inquiries were made concerning "Elizabeth Barrows." I found four letters awaiting me, each one offering me a situation if, after an interview, my appearance and qualifications were satisfactory. But I was obliged to give up all ideas of remaining longer in service, as there was other work requiring my attention. For the next few days I took advantage of every opportunity to interview mistresses and servants, trying to discover the rights and wrongs on both sides of the question. Now, having given much time and thought to the question of domestic service, I am brought to ask myself, "What have I learned by my two weeks spent in service?" I had first become interested in the subject through a conversation with a Camberwell sewing-girl, as I stated in my first chapter, and then I had always contended that domestic work was not in itself degrading, and that there was no reason why the women of the lower classes only should go out to service. I wished to find out for myself if there was anything incompatible between refinement and domestic service, and I went out as a journalist, seeking information, with the intention of giving my personal experiences.

I did not start with the idea that all mistresses were tyrants and all servants badly-treated slaves, and I do not set myself up as the champion of the "poor servant-girl." I am just as much inclined to take the part of the long-suffering mistress. In fact, from what I have seen, I have come to the conclusion that there are as many ill-treated mistresses as servants in London. I found Mrs. Allison to be an unjust and unreasonable mistress, demanding more work of her servants than she had any right to expect. With such a large and inconvenient house as hers, she needed to keep at least two strong, healthy house-maids to do the work properly. Had I, in my unfitness for the position, been the only one who had been weighed in the balance and found wanting, I should not thus take occasion to advise her; but Annie, who was a girl accustomed to hard work from her child-hood, had been obliged to exchange her place as housemaid for what she thought might be the lighter duties of parlourmaid, and her predecessor had worked herself into the hospital. Remembering this, I feel that I am right in saying that Mrs. Allison is not considerate in her treatment of her servants, neither as regards the work she requires of them nor the kind of food with which she supplies them. I am not now referring to the board wages she allowed, but to the meals which she ordered the cook to prepare for them. A breakfast of bread-and-butter and coffee is not a proper one for a servant. In fact, I do not believe anyone could accomplish satisfactory work on such fare, unless blessed with a very delicate and limited sort of appetite. The noon dinner at Mrs. Allison's was not so bad. It usually consisted of a joint, potatoes, bread, and pudding, but that was the only good meal her servants were given. For supper they had bread and cheese, day after day and week after week. It is not an excuse for Mrs. Allison to say that thousands of girls would be glad to have bread and cheese all the year round. I am aware that many women are starving in London, but that does not justify a woman in neglecting to look after the wants of those in her employ. Mistresses, hiring servants, promise to pay them a certain wage and board. Shall they give their housemaids a piece of dry bread and say, "Take and eat it, and be thankful; remembering that many girls are very hungry in the East-End and have not even a crust"?

Mrs. Brownlow, on the other hand, was kind and considerate with her servants. She gave them too much liberty, and thought more of their comfort than of her own well-being. Her house had been fitted up with a view of making the work light and easy of accomplishment, and three servants should have done all the work and had plenty of leisure for rest and recreation. Alice and the cook were most ungrateful and neglectful, and did not in any way endeavour to please. So in the face of all this, it can readily be seen that I have no reason to pose as the defender of the London servant-girls; neither am I prepared to condemn them all, and try to push them out of their situations and fill their places with another class of women.

Still, with this vexing servant problem becoming more and more important every year, it would seem that something should be done to bring about a change. There are many young women now employed as servants who are a disgrace to their trade. They have no capacity for domestic work, and are perfectly devoid of ideas as to the best way of performing their duties. Besides having no reasoning faculties, they have no sense of honour, and seem to be unable to appreciate their unfitness for such service. Just what they would be able to do, and do well, is something I have not discovered, if, indeed, there is any room at all for them on this planet. It may be that they originally had a talent for something; but, if so, it must long ago have been wrapped in a napkin and buried deep down in the earth.

Then there are girls who are eminently fitted for housework—those whose quiet inclinations would lead them to domestic labour as a means of livelihood, except for the foolish idea that in doing so they would demean themselves. So, down in the East-End, in the City, and in every direction of this great London, they are wearing out body and soul with sewing, writing in offices, factory work, and doing other things where the hours are many and the wages small, but prating ever of their "liberty" and "independence." If they get sufficient food to keep them alive and a mere covering for their bodies, it is all they can ever expect; for they are ordinary, commonplace sort of women, these toilers, and do not look forward to being experts. Many of them would make good cooks and housemaids—some of them have a special talent for just such work—but they do not think of going out to work. Why? Because they must give up their "liberty." And in what does their present liberty consist? So far as I can see, it seems to be liberty to starve.

There are young women—daughters of genteel, but poor parents—living at home, a burden to their families, doing nothing to lighten the care of their overworked fathers, sitting idly by the window doing fancy work, perhaps, waiting and watching for what? —a husband. There do not seem to be enough husbands in England to go around, and to many of these girls the desired deliverer never turns up; they live on their perfectly useless lives, a burden to everyone about them. Why have they not been trained to some sort of work and qualified to take care of themselves? Some of them would make excellent cooks and houseworkers if they had proper training. Perhaps they already know how to perform certain household duties, but to earn money by doing that work for other people they imagine would be degrading.

And now I come to a very important phase of

this subject, that of the necessity for thorough training for domestic work. I know that the orthodox belief is that all women are naturally domesticated—that they come into the world expressly to be wives, mothers, and housekeepers—and when an occasional woman seems not to get the opportunity to take such a position, something has gone wrong in the universe, and the laws have all got entangled. From what I know of womankind, I am convinced that many women are in no way fitted for domestic work, and would only be miserable if they attempted it, although their incapacity for household work and management does not necessarily prevent their being excellent wives and mothers. I will admit that many girls do have a special talent for cooking, sweeping, and dusting; but even they need to be drilled and instructed, just as a person who is a natural artist, musician, or writer needs training for the work. If all the domestic arts were taught in private and public schools, an opportunity would be given to aspirants in this line to go on and perfect themselves; while, of course, those whose tastes did not lead them in such direction, should not be obliged to take up the study. The cooking schools that have already been started in London are accomplishing a vast amount of good, but free schools for instruction in every department of household work are much needed. In advocating these schools I do not undervalue home-training. Many young women have ample opportunity to go down into their own mothers' kitchens and take lessons in domestic economy; but there are hundreds of girls who have no homes and are unable to do this, and it is for them especially that such schools are in demand.

It may be argued that with the influx of a higher class of women into domestic service, all the present servants will be thrown out of employment, and thus, while doing good to some, a great evil will be done to others. This is not likely to be the case, because the demand for good work is much greater than the supply, and there is room for both. Those men and women who insist that a person employed by them must necessarily be beneath them, and constantly show them deference as to a superior order of beings, will doubtless always cling to the present class of servants ; and then ladies who are already suited, and have no reason to dismiss their servants, are not likely to make a change. Thus it will be only the bad servants who will find it impossible to secure situations.

Another difficulty that may present itself is that it would be unpleasant for girls of refinement to be thrown in contact with servants of a lower grade in the same household. The only way out of this difficulty would be for every lady to employ only one class of domestic help. I can understand how an educated girl, obliged to work in the companionship of such girls as Annie and Alice, would find her position a most unhappy one. As a journalist out on an adventure, I was interested in studying them, and in that way my association with them was not so unpleasant ; but, had I remained a servant at Mrs. Brownlow's or Mrs. Allison's, the society of the other servants would have made me utterly miserable, and they would have cared no more for my companionship than I for theirs, as we had little in common. Ladies employing domestic helps would realise this, and so choose the kind of women they wished to have in their houses. I can see nothing in the work itself that would make it distasteful to girls of genteel birth and rearing who have domestic tendencies. In a house properly fitted up with the conveniences and comforts of modern life the work is not drudgery, and I think there is as much demand in this line for education and scientific thought as in the majority of other callings.

Now, I am not asking that all London be torn down and rebuilt to make room for a new order of servants. Houses like Mrs. Allison's might be made convenient by the expenditure of a few pounds in putting in lifts from the basement to the first floor, and fitting the bedrooms with hot- and cold-water pipes, which would do away with the necessity of carrying heavy trays and water-cans up and down the stairs. By doing this, the number of servants required would be reduced to almost half, so that it would be a matter of economy to make these improvements. The method of heating the houses might also be changed with great advantage. The insertion of hot-air furnaces or gas-grates would not entail much expense. There would not only be less work for servants, but a great stride would be made in the matter of cleanliness. It would not be necessary to heat the whole house up to the boiling-point, as Americans are accused of doing. The heat would be more easily regulated than with coal-fires, and, when the change was once made, there would be a large saving in the price of fuel.

In advocating this change in domestic workers, I do not, by any means, announce myself as being in favour of what is now known as the "lady-help." All the "lady-helps" I have met have been too much afraid of soiling their hands and hurting their dignity to accomplish good work. Quite recently one applied at my home for a situation, and her first demand was that she should be made a "member of the family." I explained that such a thing would be impossible, and she showed the greatest amazement when I informed her that on my "at-home" day she was expected to wait on my visitors, not to chat with them, and when told that she must serve the meals, instead of joining us at the family dinner, her anger knew no bounds. She went off in a huff, saying that she would not be a servant to her inferiors. It is this ridiculous way of looking at things that has created a prejudice against "lady-helps." Such help is an impossibility in a well-ordered house. The educated woman who engages as a domestic must understand that there is no question as to her inferiority or superiority. If she works for a woman who is far below her socially and intellectually, she may retain her self-respect just the same. Her employer—I would abolish the terms "master" and "mistress" in this connection, as savouring of slavery days—does not ask her to become her companion or a member of the family. Such an arrangement might prove very unpleasant on either side. It is simply a business arrangement, a question of employer and employee. In answer to my advertisement for a situation, I received a few letters from women who wished me to be a "daughter" to them; but, as I had not advertised for a mother, I considered such propositions in very bad taste, and felt sure that no intelligent women would have written me such letters. The educated housemaid would be employed for the same purpose as the uneducated one. Her business is to sweep the floor, make the beds, and do other household work, just the same as the other class would do. No, not the same either, for she should do her work better. The educated parlourmaid will not sit down at the family dinner ; she is hired to wait at the table. Her employer is under no obligations to invite her to sit in her boudoir or introduce her to her friends. She is paid money for value received. Each must respect the other. That is the whole thing in a nutshell. I believe that if educated women would take up this matter in a proper way great good would come of it, not only to themselves, but to the "working-girls" of London.

And what shall be done about the cap and apron, the "Yes, ma'am," and the "No, sir"? If I were in service the matter of cap and apron would be of little importance to me so long as the costume was becoming. I cannot see why exception should be taken to such a very pretty bit of headgear as the ruffled cap. The girl in the cap looks much neater than the one without it, and it seems to be particularly appropriate for domestic work. During my two weeks in service my self-respect did not diminish in the least. Yet I think that if some members of the new order of house and parlourmaids insist on the abolition of the cap, they will find as many ladies who will not make it a question of prime importance. Surely, no one going out as a cook would object to wearing a head covering which is merely indicative of neatness while preparing the food. So far as the apron is concerned, a sensible girl will see at a glance that it is a positively necessary article of apparel, and is no more a "badge" of anything demeaning than is the small silk or white apron often worn by ladies when doing fancy work. As for the "ma'am" and the "sir," I think we might dispense with them without much loss, so long as proper respect is shown on both sides. A lady employing a person whom she knew was her social and intellectual equal would naturally expect to make certain changes in little things like this, and the improved kind of service would, I am sure, more than make up for the loss of a "Yes, ma'am."

What about "followers"? Shall young ladies employed as domestics be obliged to walk on the street or go in the parks in order to meet their friends and sweathearts? Certainly not. They must have the use of a comfortable sitting-room, where they may receive visitors on certain afternoons or evenings, the number of their callers and the length of their stay being kept, of course, within the bounds of reason. The present class of servant-girls have much cause for complaint on this score. To stipulate that a girl shall have no visitors is as unkind as it is unreasonable and dangerous. A young woman servant is quite likely to have friends of both sexes, and it is probable that she is "keeping company." To compel her future husband to hang over the area-fence whistling for her to come out, or to oblige her to go to the park and sit on the benches in order to have a talk with him, is not only inconsiderate, it is almost indecent. She should be allowed to receive him once a week or once a fortnight in the servant's hall. It is not difficult to arrange this matter satisfactorily if reason is shown on the part of both employer and employed.

However, taking service as it is at present, I think that the position of a domestic servant with a reasonable mistress and in a conveniently-arranged house is far superior to that of the sewing-girl, the factory-girl, or the struggling stenographer and book-keeper in the City. There are hundreds of places like Mrs. Brownlow's, where employment can be found for girls who are not receiving the much-discussed "living wage," and for those girls, surely, domestic work is preferable to their present employ-ment. There are kind, thoughtful, and considerate women in London who would appreciate good servants and pay fair wages for work well done. There are also, I know, hundreds of girls who are especially fitted for rendering this service. I wish they could be brought to view this subject from a philosophical standpoint, and I would use my influence to convince them that all labour, well performed, is elevating, not demeaning ; that the woman who bakes a loaf of bread properly, polishes the family plate so that it may be mistaken for a mirror, or scrubs the kitchen table white and clean, giving her heart and best talents to the work, is as worthy of respect and praise as the painter who depicts on canvas the glories of the sunlit landscape, the poet who weaves his thoughts into verse, or the sovereign who reigns on a throne.

THE "ALMIGHTY DOLLAR" IN LONDON SOCIETY.

CHAPTER I.

ADVERTISING FOR A CHAPERON.

AMERICANS are accused of having a too implicit confidence in the purchasing power of their country's coin. In fact, certain foreigners have been known to say that the God referred to in the motto, "In God we trust," engraved on the silver dollar, is in reality a deity of white metal designed and fashioned at the United States Mint.

"The trouble with your people," said an Englishman to me recently, "is that you put too much value on money. It is a convenient article, I will admit; but you seem to have an idea that you can do anything with it."

"And, pray, will you give me a list of the things money will not buy in England as well as in America?" I replied.

"Well, for instance," he answered, "take birth and position. You have an aristocracy of money in America. Here we have one of blood, where pounds, shillings, and pence are not taken into consideration."

"Ah, indeed!" I responded, "I don't know anything about the pounds, shillings, and pence feature

H

of the case; but I am inclined to think that our dollars and cents are something of a social factor over here."

My English friend—bless his dear old aristocratic heart!—appeared to be greatly shocked at my suggestion, and assured me that I was mistaken. I longed for facts with which to confront him, and, having faith in advertising as a means of getting anything that one is willing to pay for, I wrote out an advertisement, which the next day appeared in the personal columns of a prominent London paper. Thus it ran :—

A YOUNG AMERICAN LADY of means wishes to meet with a Chaperon of Highest Social Position, who will introduce her into the Best English Society. Liberal terms. Address, "Heiress,"——.

Two days later, calling at the office of an advertising agency on Piccadilly, I found eighty-seven letters (needless to remark that there were no post-cards) in answer to my advertisement. I had offers from every fashionable neighbourhood in London. Park Lane, Cavendish Square, Grosvenor Square, South Kensington, West Kensington, all were represented; and the thoughtlessness of the writers in signing their full names and titles to their epistles was something that surprised me. However, nearly every letter was marked at the top "Confidential," "Private," or "Personal," and it seemed to be an understood thing that the affair should go no further. The confidence they exhibited in the "honour" of a total stranger was rather remarkable. Still, I hope the applicants will forgive me if, after having, in the kindness of my heart, kept their real names out of print, I am now tempted to publish some of their correspondence. Here is a copy of one of the letters :—

"*Private.*]

"Madam,—In answer to your advertisement, I beg to say that I have a very charming house at the above excellent address, which, in itself, would almost insure you a good social position. I speak of this, thinking that you, being an American, may not be aware that a good London address is of much importance in a social way to one whose position is not already established by birth. I am the widow of a well-known English officer—the late Sir Blankety Blank—of whom you have doubtless heard, and I am also titled in my own right. My position is assured, and I can introduce you to the very best people in England, and present you at Court at the first Drawing Room. I could take you into my home next spring, or we could travel together during the winter and return to London at the beginning of the season. I would suggest that you spend the winter months, or part of them, in the South of France, where you would meet the most fashionable people. It may be of interest to you to know that I chaperoned Miss Porkolis, of Chicago, three years ago, and introduced her at Court, although she did not reside with me, as her mother took a furnished house in London for the season. I can give you good references as to my standing, and would require in return a solicitor's and banker's references as to your financial position.

"My terms in London for three months in the spring would be £200 per month, which would include board and residence. If you decided to travel, the terms while on the Continent would be £100 per month, you to pay the travelling and hotel expenses for both. Of course, you would also be expected to defray such expenses as carriage-hire, a maid, &c. In thinking over these terms, you must take into consideration that I offer you exceptional advantages.—Very truly yours,

"A. B. C., Lady ——."

In reading this letter, I was particularly struck with the fact that the writer, although she required my banker's and solicitor's reference as to my financial standing, asked for no voucher for my respectability and position in my own country. She was ready to bargain to introduce me not only to the best English society, but to the Queen herself, for upwards of

H 2

£1,000, or something over 5,000 dols. in American money. I agreed with her that the advantages she had to offer were exceptional. The name the lady gave was one well known to me, and I was aware that she was not exaggerating when she spoke of her position in society. I had also the honour of a passing acquaintance with Miss Porkolis, whom she mentioned as having chaperoned. Hiring the use of a private letter-box, I wrote Lady —— a letter couched in the following terms :—

"DEAR MADAM,—In reply to your letter, I think it only honourable that I should tell you something of myself before making an appointment to see you. I am an American girl, an orphan of considerable means, and am willing to pay liberally for what I require. I should, of course, give you the best of references in regard to my financial qualifications, and would even pay you a part of the money in advance ; but before meeting you I must be frank enough to inform you that although I myself am fairly educated and of presentable appearance, nearly all the members of my family are ordinary people, with little or no refinement and education. But, of course, none of them are in Europe, and you would never need come in contact with them. My father owned large ranches out West, and when he died, three years ago, left me the bulk of his fortune. I do not think there is anything about me that would lead you to feel ashamed of me ; but I feel it my duty to tell you that, so far as the rest of my family are concerned, they are what in my country would be termed as ' common as dirt.'

"Your terms are not higher than I should expect them to be. I like the idea of travelling in France ; and when I returned to England I should want you to give some very elegant receptions and balls for me—I, of course, to bear all expense connected with them.

"As I have told you so much about my private affairs, I would not care to give my name and address until I again hear from you, and know that you would be willing to undertake my chaperonage and introduction at Court under such circumstances as I have mentioned. If you answer in the affirmative, I will make an appointment for you to meet me at my hotel, where I am staying with my maid.—I am, Madam, very truly yours,

"—— Library, Regent Street, W.　　　　　　　"E. L. B.

The next day I received this note :—

"Lady —— presents her compliments to E. L. B., and begs to say that she can see no reason why she should not act as her chaperon, provided E. L. B. is herself a refined young lady and can furnish the reference previously referred to from her solicitor and banker. Lady —— will be pleased if E. L. B. will make an early appointment for a meeting at her hotel.'

That was the end of my negotiations with Lady ——. Her answer to my very frank avowal of my family connections certainly proved that she cared little for my ancestry or antecedents, so long as I could furnish the necessary number of dollars.

CHAPTER II.

OFFERS OF MARRIAGE.

ALTHOUGH I had intended that my advertisement should appeal to lady chaperons only, I received some rather flattering offers from members of the opposite sex. One of the most interesting of the letters was from a gentleman matrimonially inclined. Here it is word for word :—

" Will the young American lady who has just put an advertisement in the paper relative to her desire to meet an English chaperon of high social position, allow the writer of this letter to address a few lines to her and, as Americans are always candid and outspoken, permit me to be the same? May I ask you to consider over what I write, and pe haps your advertisement may be the means of working out our mutual good.

" Possibly you may desire to enter London society with the idea of what is called 'settling yourself. You may be more or less alone in England; and perhaps you like this country, its society, and customs. You would possibly desire to marry an Englishman of high social position, who could place you in a certain circle where you would *lead* others. I am a man who holds a first-rate position. I am a country gentlemen, have a fine place, house, and estate, have been an officer in a distinguished regiment, and know many people of position and rank. I am just at present in London ; and if you think it would be worth your trouble to at least talk the matter over, I would treat you with all honour and respect. This would, of course, include silence. On the other hand, it would be an absolute necessity that you should be a lady of *considerable* fortune ; and when I mention this, I trust that you will not judge me until you know my reasons for thus putting it. Whatever fortune you have would be always your own.

"If you think well of what I have written you, I would be most happy to meet you at whatever time you may appoint, at your own residence or elsewhere. Then judge me and see what manner of man I am."

This communication bore the stamp of a well-known West-End Club. In my answer I hinted that, although I had not advertised for a husband, I was not adverse to considering the matter to which he had so delicately alluded. Having a desire to follow up the affair, I engaged a room at a certain fashionable hotel for a day, and made an appointment for the gentleman to call. On the afternoon appointed I awaited him in the drawing-room of the hotel. I wore a stylish-looking costume, various pieces of showy jewellery, and a pair of diamond ear-rings, thinking to impress my would-be husband with a sense of my wealth.

At four o'clock in the afternoon my suitor made his appearance. He was a fine-looking aristocratic man of middle age. His manners were refined and elegant, and I could not help thinking that I was dealing with neither a fool nor a knave, but with a thorough English gentlemen. We had half an hour's chat, in which my social aspirations were discussed in the

most business-like manner. I did not give my real
name, neither did my companion tell me his own.
I addressed him by the assumed name he had signed
in his letter. He informed me that he was a widower
of excellent position, but that he was somewhat financially embarrassed. He wished to marry a lady of

"HE WISHED TO MARRY A LADY OF WEALTH."

wealth, and for the use of her money he was willing
to give her his name and a good social position.

Afterwards I made some investigations in regard
to the man; and to my surprise I found that he
was exactly what he represented himself to be: a
country gentleman of titled family, who was anxious
to recuperate his decaying fortunes by marrying an

heiress—an American girl preferred. I discovered his real name and address, and since my interview with him I have often seen his name mentioned in the society columns of the papers. He is still unmarried, and I suppose is still looking for a wife. So here is an opportunity for one of our American heiresses to purchase not only an introduction at Court but a husband with mortgaged estates in the bargain.

All the men who wrote seemed to hold the opinion that, as a rich American girl, my chief desire must be to capture an English husband. Not every one was so outspoken as the writer of the epistle I have just quoted ; but their letters contained either direct or indirect proposals of marriage, provided that, after a meeting, I proved to be personally and financially acceptable. From one of the scions of the nobility came the following missive, penned on violet-scented paper :—

" Mr. X. presents his compliments to ' Heiress,' who advertised this morning for a chaperon, and begs to say that he would feel honoured by a reply to this letter.   Mr. X. is the third son of the late ——, of whom the young lady has doubtless heard.   He is twenty-nine years old, of good appearance, and has served as an officer in the army. Mr. X. would much like to arrange for a meeting with the young lady, to whom he would show every courtesy, and might be able to suggest a way by which she could even more than gratify her ambition for a place in English society.   He would be also pleased to give her the best references in regard to his character as well as his high social standing.   A letter from ' Heiress' would be treated in all confidence by Mr. X."

I had no need to investigate into the genuineness of the foregoing. I happened to have seen Mr. X.'s handwriting before. In fact, he had once been presented to me at the home of a mutual acquaintance. I did not answer his letter, but consigned it to the embers of my study fire.

On paper of the finest quality, ornamented with a family crest of considerable dimensions, Mrs. Two-stars presented her compliments and begged to say that she would be happy to entertain the idea of chaperoning the young American lady and give her a delightful, cheerful home. Mrs. T., as well as her four daughters, had been presented at Court. The daughters had all married well, and their proud mother felt no compunction in saying that she thought she could introduce the young American lady to many gentlemen of birth and title, if not of fortune. She moved in excellent society, and was fond of entertaining. Terms for London season and presentation, £500, or 2,500 dols. Mrs. Twostars enclosed her photograph, a portrait of herself in her Drawing-Room gown, which, by the way, had a button off the front. The photograph was returned in the stamped and addressed envelope thoughtfully enclosed. The lady proved to be the daughter of a distinguished baronet, and the wife of a man well known in London society.

Lady So-and-So, of Queen's Gate, wrote that she would be glad to chaperon me. Terms £600 to £800 sterling, according to arrangements and the advantages required.

The Countess de Blank was also open to an engagement. She was an Englishwoman married to a foreign title.

A certain dowager of exalted rank, well known on two continents, informed me that she would undertake my chaperonage, and would hire a furnished house for me near Park Lane ; the rent would be not less than £50 per week during the season. Her own place was in the country, and she had given up her town house. She would devote her whole attention to the management of the establishment, and would introduce me as her young American friend or distant relative, if I desired. Besides the house-rent, I must bear the entire expense of keeping up the place, giving balls, theatre-parties, &c., and the dowager herself would expect the sum of £2,000 for her services. I supposed these figures were not remarkably high for a lady of so much " position," and, having some curiosity to make her acquaintance, I wrote asking for an appointment to call.

CHAPTER III.

WHAT IT WOULD COST.

ON the day appointed I started out to call on the lady who had intimated her willingness to chaperon me for £2,000. It was with considerable self-confidence that I stepped from a smart brougham before the door of her aristocratic abode, for I carried with me the assurance of my dressmaker that I looked a veritable Western heiress just from Paris ; and, the matter of dress being satisfactorily arranged, I felt no doubt as to my ability to carry out the *rôle* I had undertaken to play. The Dowager Lady —— was particularly gracious. She was not by any means

such a cold-blooded bargainer as I had imagined her
to be—that is, she did not look it. A more aristocratic, refined, and interesting woman I had never
met. She candidly explained that she was in great
need of money, and obliged to either increase her
income or diminish her expenses. Unlike one of my
other correspondents, she was unable to refer me to
any American girl whom she had chaperoned, as
she had never before attempted to make money
out of her social position ; but she assured me
that some of her friends made such use of their
influence, and she saw no reason why she should
not do the same. We discussed the *pros* and *cons*
of the matter over our tea. I was promised not only
a social position, but a husband. Just who the gentleman was my hostess did not say ; but she knew he
could be secured. But not for the £2,000. Oh no !
That sum of money would take me only so far as
Buckingham Palace. In fact, it would not even take
me there ; for, besides my chaperon's salary, I must
pay the house-rent, carriage-hire, with such inci-
dentals as butchers' and bakers' bills and other little
accessories that in three months would certainly
amount to considerably over £1,000. Then there was
my wardrobe. The lady suggested that it would need
refurnishing, and she knew of a wonderfully clever
West-End dressmaker. There were also the presentation dress, the bouquets, *boutonnières* for the
coachmen, a string of pearls for my neck, because they
would be girlish and simple, and all that ; for these
and many more things another £1,000 would not go
too far.

"And how much do you charge for the husband ?"

was the abrupt question I felt inclined to put. But I only said sweetly, " If I really got married, I would not forget you, of course." She answered laughingly, " You might make me a present, you know."

So the result of my interview was, that I was to pay out between £4,000 and £5,000 for a "season" in London, introductions into the best society, and a presentation at Court. It was more than probable that during my career as a society belle, some poor though perhaps fascinating young, middle-aged, or old nobleman (no matter what his age so long as his lineage was correct) would fall deeply in love with me, lured on possibly by my chaperon's representations concerning the state of my cattle-ranches out West. Then I would marry him and be an ornament to society, and I would give Lady —— a little present of a cheque or a house in Park Lane, or even some land in the far Western State, where my herds grazed peacefully on a thousand hills. Surely the purchasing power of the "almighty dollar" was not to be despised !

Thinking to further increase my fund of information, I answered several advertisements that seemed to refer to the scheme I had taken in hand, In the financial column of a morning paper I found this :—

A LADY OF TITLE wishes to borrow £1,000 for six months. Would act as chaperon to young lady.

I wrote to the address given, repeating my American heiress story. I stated that I was looking for a chaperon, and was willing to *give*, instead of *lend*, £1,000 to the proper person. My answer came from a solicitor's office. It read :—

" MADAM,—My client, feeling, as you do, the delicacy that exists in the matter, has handed to me your letter of the 10th inst., and has desired me to communicate with you thereon. There is no question that she is in a position to do what you desire ; and, as it is somewhat difficult to arrive at any conclusion by correspondence, I would suggest that you allow me to meet you with the view of thoroughly discussing the matter. I should be glad to see you either at my office or your house ; or, indeed, as ladies are admitted at the —— Club during the hour of afternoon tea, it might be convenient if the interview took place there, where, without any undue observation, I could arrange a meeting with my client."

Other advertisements to which I replied were somewhat of this kind :—

> A LADY OF GOOD POSITION, speaking several languages, expects to spend the winter on the Continent, and is willing to chaperon one or two young girls and receive them into her home on her return to London.

When I wrote to the advertisers, most of them stated that they would prefer an American girl to travel and live with them.

At the beginning of my investigations, I did not start out with a lantern searching for an honest man ; but I think I found him by answering this advertisement :—

> A FAMILY OF GOOD POSITION will give Board and Residence to Young Lady in West-End. Will chaperon her if desired.

In reply to the letter, in which I frankly confided all my social aspirations, I received a note that seemed likely to destroy one of the most valuable commercial qualities that I, as a journalist, had hitherto possessed —my cynicism. Here it is :—

" DEAR MADAM,—Under the peculiar circumstances, I am sure it will be better that we commence our negotiations by showing mutual trust in each other. I therefore give you my full address and write in my own name, feeling sure that you will appreciate my motives, and keep the knowledge to yourself. You can readily understand that in our position we do not want the matter to become public property or the subject of talk.

"My wife could, I think, introduce you into *good* English society, but not into *titled* society, which I know is aimed at by many American ladies, but in reality is only gained by the assistance of the needy nobility—mostly dowagers with small means and 'marketable handles' to their names.

"You, I think, will see that it is not practicable to give exact terms, as you asked for in your letter, without much more information than can be given in any letter, however explicit. Could you arrange, therefore, to call here at any time (we do not object to a Sunday) and see my wife and myself, when doubtless we might come to some pleasant arrangements and understanding?"

Oh, Diogenes! what a pity you did not read the advertising columns of the morning papers!

With the exception of the one honest man whose letter I have quoted, none of those with whom I had negotiations refused to entertain my proposition, even when I acknowledged my deplorable lack of ancestry and proper family connections. The large fortune I represented myself as possessing seemed to cover a multitude of embarrassing circumstances, if not positive sins. Had I carried my experiment further and been introduced and presented at Court, I should only have been one of numerous Americans who have walked on a golden pavement to the Throne Room of Buckingham Palace.

CHAPTER IV.

INTERESTING ANTECEDENTS.

IT may be of interest to English readers to know something concerning my countrywomen who have made a sensation during a London season. Many of them are unknown, or at least unrecognised, by the best American society.

Take Miss Porkolis, for example, the Western girl whom Lady —— spoke of having chaperoned. Her grandfather was interested in the lard business, and who her great-grandfather was history sayeth not. The present Mr. Porkolis has retired to a country house and lives on his income. When Miss Porkolis was introduced to London society she was even in a worse state than I represented myself to be ; for not only were the members of her family unrefined and uneducated, but the young lady herself made the most startling blunders in grammar and spelling. No wonder that Lady ——, in considering my proposition, made the proviso that I myself must be possessed of some refinement and education. She was doubtless thinking of the many embarrassments she suffered during the career of Miss Porkolis !

There were the Cole-Kings, two sisters, chaperoned by a well-known social star. Both were beautiful, fascinating, and wealthy. They were from the Wild West, but were educated in an Eastern seminary, and then sent to a "finishing school" to be polished off. The polishing process lasted over two years ; and then, after a vain attempt to number themselves among the New York "Four Hundred," they made a trip over the Continent, and turned up in London in time for the festivities of the season.

The Diamondsons came over *en famille*, and entertained magnificently in London not a dozen years ago. Everybody went to their " crushes," because with them money seemed to be no object. In speaking of the British and American monetary system one time, Mr. Diamondson was heard to remark that, although he generally thought in dollars, he would just as soon pay out pounds as dollars, as it was simply a matter of multiplication by five anyhow. So when Miss Evelyn Diamondson wanted a dress from Messrs. Swagger and Swell, it made no difference to her adoring father whether it cost one hundred dollars or one hundred pounds. It was, then, not surprising that, with all their recklessness as regarded the expenditure of money, the Diamondsons became immensely popular. Their daughter *almost* married a man of high degree in England, and then *quite* married a titled foreigner—a harmless sort of person, who contentedly spends the income allowed him by his father-in-law.

I could give a long list of my recently Anglicised countrypeople who in England are mistakenly looked upon as fair specimens of America's best citizens. There are the Snobsons, of wheat farm fame; the Candlemans, who grew opulent on the proceeds of their tallow and fat business ; and the Welldiggers, who awoke one morning to find themselves millionaires, one of the " hired men " having "struck oil " on the outskirts of the farm after the rest of the family had gone to bed. Mr. Welldigger took the hired man into partnership, and proposed that he should marry Angelica, his only daughter. But Angelica positively declined, having made up her mind to cross the ocean and marry a title, which she did, and greatly to her credit too, for never a girl fished harder with gilded bait than did Angelica.

The prevalence of French names and hyphens among the signatures of rich Americans has often been remarked upon. About the first thing that occurs to a man with newly-acquired wealth and social aspirations is to make some sort of change in his name, if it happens to be an unfashionable one, which is often the case. If Patrick Rafferty becomes a millionaire by a sudden speculation, either he or his wife will immediately discover that the family is really of French origin, and that the name should be pronounced *Raffertay*, with the accent on the last syllable; while if Luther Jones determines to attempt to scale the social ladder in London, he will have new cards engraved, which will read thus: "Mr. Luther-Jones." Then the French "de" is also quite popular among our would-be aristocrats, and such names as "de Brown" and "de Smithers" are considered quite the thing for a family about to make a European trip.

And yet, "what's in a name?" So far as society is concerned, the daughters of the men I have mentioned would have experienced no difficulty in finding chaperons to introduce them in London even if their names had been plain Jones or Smithers, so long as they paid the price, which I have discovered is made according to the advantages offered.

So, after all my investigations, my faith in the purchasing power of the "Almighty Dollar" still remains unshaken.

I

THE PRICE OF A PEDIGREE.

WHEN General Harrison was running for the Presidency, the members of the opposition party looked about for a slur to cast upon him. Finally, they brought forward an accusation of the gravest possible kind. It was that the poor man had a grandfather, which, being altogether un-American, proved conclusively that he ought never to be elected President of the United States. During that campaign many good Democrats put the pictures of their ancestors away in the attic, or turned them with faces towards the wall, in order to escape the imputation of being traitors to Democratic principles. In certain circles it was looked upon as nothing short of a crime to have a family-tree and to be able to tell with any degree of certainty from which branch one had sprouted.

I do not know whether General Harrison's election had anything to do with making grandfathers more popular, but for the past few years I have noticed that not only grandfathers, but ancestors removed many generations back, were getting immensely fashionable, especially among people of suddenly-acquired wealth. It has often occurred to me that there must be some sort of mill or shop where forefathers and coats-of-arms were made to order. I have known persons who one month wrote on plain

I 2

note-paper, drove in hired hansoms, and had the walls of the "parlour" adorned with chromos, who the next month indited notes on stationery embossed with strangely-wrought characters in gold and bronze and purple, and invited their friends to call at a new house, where, on the drawing-room walls, hung old-fashioned gilded frames, from which stared cracked and battered portraits of men and women of ancient times. I have always noticed that the advent of these things was simultaneous with a rise in the price of pork, the finding of a new mine, or a hitherto undiscovered oil-well.

Some years ago a young New York lawyer, who, had he lived in England, would have been known as a "briefless barrister," confided to me that he wished to go to one of the Western States and start in his profession, but he was kept back for the lack of a few hundred dollars. He was clever, talented, and had boundless ambition, the sort of man that always rises in America. He had been an only son, but his parents had left him no legacy, except an honoured name and a family-tree of considerable dimensions. One day, in talking over his resources, a sudden thought occurred to him, and his face brightened.

"Do you know," said he, "it seems as if those ancestors of mine ought to be worth something to me in a crisis like this!"

"But they're not," I answered. "You know they're as dead as a door-nail. There's nothing for you but to go and saw wood."

Still he persisted that ancestors were realisable assets, if he could only find a market for them, and ex-plained that many a rich man would be glad to own such a pedigree and coat-of-arms as he possessed. The next day he brought a parcel of papers, which contained a full account of his genealogy, a description of his ancestral halls, and a crest of no mean order ; and, going over them, he made it clear to me just how, with a few slight changes, everything might be made to apply to almost any person and fit the case exactly.

At first I was shocked, and could not enter into the spirit of the thing, though I could not but admire his resourceful mind. There seemed to be something uncanny and sacrilegious about selling off one's forefather's like that, and I told him so, comparing him to Esau, who sold his birthright for a mess of pottage.

I went to South America soon afterwards, and thought no more about the affair until three or four months ago I received a marked copy of a Western paper, which spoke of the fame recently achieved by a rising young lawyer, who was one of the coming men of the great West. It was my old-time friend, and I fell to wondering whether he had realised a sufficient amount on his pedigree to enable him to make the start he wanted. I wrote, asking him if he had succeeded in disposing of his heritage, and also desired him to give me any additional information he could in regard to modern genealogical matters. A few weeks later I had a letter from him, stating that, soon after I left New York, he had found a buyer for his wares in the person of a wealthy citizen of Dakota, who, happening to have the same name as his own (which was not an uncommon one), paid him $800 down cash, and was not even put to the

trouble of making any changes.   At the close of his
letter he wrote :—

"You probably have not heard that the Highfliers, of Wyoming,
have suddenly come out with a coat-of-arms and weird-looking old oil-
paintings.   I have taken the pains to investigate it for you, and I understand that they had some private person, who lives near London, to
attend to the matter for them.   The coat-of-arms is not genuine, I am
sure, and the paintings, though doubtless somebody's ancestors, are
not their own.   You might go and see the man in the interest of your
profession.   His address is ——.   As for myself, I am getting on
swimmingly since I sold my birthright, and when anyone inquires into
the details of my forbears, I put them off with the quotation :

" ' The rank is but the guinea stamp,
    The man's the man for a' that.' "

The place indicated was in one of the suburbs of
London, and I called twice at the address before I
found the person I sought.   The gentility and un-
pretentious bearing of the house I visited rather disappointed me ; for I half-expected to see a shop with
crests, stamps, and trees displayed in the window, and
suspended over the door some such sign as " Pedigrees While You Wait."

The man who answered to the name my friend
had given me was also a disappointment.   He
did not have the appearance of a manufacturer of
ancestors and armorial ensigns.   He was a thorough
gentleman, but not like an Englishman.   He seemed
to be of German extraction, though he spoke without
an accent.

I explained that I was an American, and was
anxious to obtain some information concerning my
father's people, who were English.   I gave my name
as Miss Helen Simpkins.   I think the name must
have discouraged him at once ; for he put on an

exceedingly doubtful look, as if wondering whether any good could come out of the Simpkinses or, rather, if the Simpkinses could have come out of any good. The name certainly did not have an aristocratic ring about it. That was why I gave it. I thought it quite as good as Highflier, and likely to bring about just as satisfactory results.

"Simpkins, Simpkins," he repeated in a musing sort of way. "Is that an old English name?"

"I don't know how old it is," I answered, "but it is my name, and my father's people were English. I want to find out who they were and what they were. I understand that you make investigations of this kind for Americans."

"Yes," he answered, with the semblance of a smile. "I have sometimes done that, as I am interested in the study of genealogy and the subject of heredity, though I do not make a business of it. Yet I have helped some of your country people in that way."

"How much does it cost?" I asked bluntly.

"Well, my charge, of course, depends upon the trouble I am obliged to take. I suppose you have some information to give me concerning your grandfather, great-grandfather, where they lived, whether they were what is known as gentlemen, and when they went to America? It may be a very simple matter, in which case the cost would be trifling—not more than five or six guineas."

He seemed so genuine, so honest, and withal such a gentleman, that I began to believe he never could have helped the Highfliers in their quest of a lineage

"You see," said I, "my father and mother are not living, and, as I am the only member of the family, I have no means of finding out anything concerning my father's ancestors, except that I know his father was named Samuel Simpkins and lived somewhere in England. I thought you could hunt all that up for me ; and I was prepared to pay you for your trouble, whatever you might ask."

I spoke in a melancholy, innocent sort of tone, and my auditor smiled good-naturedly, as he said :

" I am afraid I could not do anything with such vague information as you have at your command, even though you gave me a thousand pounds. We must have something to start on, and you have nothing. If you are a wealthy American lady, as I suppose you are, I would not, if I were you, bother myself about questions of this sort. Indeed, you have no necessity to trouble about ancestors. To be an American woman is honour enough."

He was so very kind and so American-like in his gallantry, that I felt like confessing myself a sham ; but the thought of Henrietta Highflier, and all the airs she had doubtless assumed with her new-found dignity, induced me to make another effort before giving up.

" I am so sorry ; I thought you could help me. I understood that you did something for the Highfliers, of Wyoming. Did Mr. Highflier know anything more about his grandfathers than I know about mine ? "

He smiled when I mentioned the name of Highflier.

" Yes, I did put myself to considerable trouble for the Highfliers," he answered ; " but theirs was a peculiar case."

" Mine is also a peculiar case. It is not pleasant

to know nothing about one's people. I have come to England purposely to find out, and I don't like to go back to America with no more information than when I came. I am willing to pay anything you ask for the trouble I make you. I have no one to care what I do with my money." I was anxious to get away from this very pleasant man, but still I must know about the Highfliers.

"Is it then for America only that you wish a coat-of-arms and a genealogical-table? You do not intend to remain in England or on the Continent?"

"Yes, I want something to show my American friends, a crest for the brougham and stamp for my note paper. I do not expect to stop in England after this month," was my reply.

"Very well," he said. "I can supply you with what you seem to want for two hundred pounds, if you desire to spend your money so foolishly. I will be perfectly honest with you and tell you that it will be better for you to use the crest only in America where people will not put it to a close scrutiny. You had best think the matter over before you decide. You look intelligent and I think you can understand my position in the matter. I am always honourable in my dealings."

"Did you arrange it that way for the Highfliers?" I asked, making my final stroke, as I prepared to leave.

"I am hardly at liberty to answer your question," he replied with great dignity.

He shook hands, and bowed me out in a kindly, fatherly sort of way. I could not help but admire the genuineness of the man who did not attempt to

pass off a sham thing for a real. If rich Americans
were willing to pay him a thousand dollars for drawing original pictures of trees, animals, and coronets
and making a list of names on paper or attaching
them to the branches of an apple-tree, knowing the
while that they were pictures only, nobody could
blame him for amusing himself and accepting the
money.

After my interview with the man who did the
Highfliers such an inestimable service, I discovered
another person in the City who, without troubling
me with embarrassing questions concerning the
Simpkinses of a past age, would undertake to provide
me with a noble line of ancestors extending back
several generations, his charges to be according to the
length of the line. This was reasonable enough ; for,
of course, the larger the number of ancestors, the
more time and thought spent in the investigation, or
manufacture, as the case might be. I considered
this plan of supplying forefathers at so much a head
the only true business-like way of carrying out such
a transaction. If I cared for a pedigree to begin
with the thirteenth, fourteenth, or fifteenth century,
the price would naturally be higher than one which
started in the seventeenth or eighteenth century.
The lowest price for which any investigation would
be undertaken was £50, while a coat-of-arms would
be "authenticated" for £10 extra. I presume that
this price would be increased if I demanded anything
of a very elaborate order.

Those who study the advertising columns of the
daily papers have doubtless often noticed the advertisement of a "private gentleman," who advises

Americans and others that he is prepared to authenticate pedigrees and emblazon escutcheons at reasonable terms. Many of my countrypeople who visit London during the season have received from this gentleman neatly-engraved cards, stating that he makes a speciality of the study of heraldry in connection with the stationery business. He says that many Americans, though they know it not, can really trace their families back to the blood royal of England. But this gentleman's customers are not all Americans. He has been patronised by numbers of City men and tradespeople of London, who, with the acquisition of wealth made in stockbroking or the drapery trade, feel a sudden craving for knowledge of their ancestry. Many of them are so deceived by the pedigree-maker that they believe the strange, weird tales he tells them, while others are satisfied to make their neighbours believe them.

The genealogies thus supplied are probably quite as genuine as many of those collected together in certain books relating to the existing gentle and noble families of England. In looking over these publications, I have often been struck with the fact that nearly all the pedigrees commence with the time of Conquest, and I have been surprised to find that nearly everybody worth mentioning had ancestors who were "close friends" of William the Conqueror. It is wonderful the number of intimate companions that crusty old invader had! According to the genealogical records, they were more numerous than the sands of the desert. In some of these pedigrees there seem to have been at times several generations that got lost in some unaccountable way, so that in many instances it would appear that certain men must have been the sons of their great-great-grandfathers, unless, like Topsy, they "just growed." Such discrepancies as these are doubtless due to the stupidity of pedigree-makers who lived two or three centuries ago, and they have been allowed to go on uncorrected. Nineteenth-century genealogists know their business better, and they go on the principle that "what is worth doing at all is worth doing well;" hence a pedigree now made to order reads smoothly and consistently, and the possessor may congratulate himself on the fact that he is able to secure the very latest thing in this line.

Some genealogists have been known to show a sense of the eternal fitness of things by supplying their customers with crests and arms to suit their particular vocations. A few years ago a wealthy Chicago pork-dealer, who had expressed his willingness to pay a large sum of money for a crest and family-tree, was much insulted on receiving a sheet of paper stamped with a picture of three wild boars standing on their hind legs. He refused to pay for it on the ground that it was too personal, and now his carriage panels are ornamented with a crest of an entirely different character. If people would only be more consistent in such matters, the art of heraldry might be put to much greater use than it is at present; but consistency is so costly a jewel that there are few who can afford to wear it. How convenient it would be if Miss Brewer, of Milwaukee, would have the top of her note-paper embellished with a drawing of a brightly-coloured cask or barrel! On the family plate of the wealthy Dakota farmer might be engraved a sheaf of

wheat, while the escutcheon of the Pennsylvania
coal baron could be adorned with a representation of
a glowing furnace.

In these days of the " new woman," the " new journalism," the " new drama," and the " new art," I am
surprised that someone does not invent something
original in the way of pedigrees, and call it the " new
heraldry." Cannot a man be found who is bold
and honest enough to start his pedigree in the latter
part of the nineteenth century, commencing with himself, and taking for his coat-of-arms the symbol of his
own trade or profession? Such a course would be
the only proper one for so-called " self-made " men to
adopt, both in England and America. In such a case,
a very appropriate motto would be " Every Man His
Own Ancestor."

But until such a person comes forward, I suppose
we shall have to put up with such improvements and
conveniences as we already have, which, after all,
are not to be despised. " Made ancestors " possess
peculiar advantages over the genuine articles, inas-
much as they may be manufactured at notice to suit
all tastes and requirements. Then, too, the plan, to
a great extent, does away with the family skeletons
of a past generation, which are always liable to pop
up at inopportune times and create embarrassments.
According to the present method, anybody with
money may be descended from knights, earls, dukes,
and even kings, all of the best variety and irreproach-
able character. Crests of colours and designs most
pleasing to the eye may always be obtained, and the
coat of mail that stands in the hall may be ever
bright and new.

Those plebeians who insist on pedigrees of ancient date may be accommodated by entering into negotiations with the aristocratic poor of all countries, and even persons with genealogies and crests of their own are privileged to have them altered and rearranged at pleasure. In this connection I am reminded of the story of a Boston lady, who, visiting London recently, decided to go to a sort of private heraldic bureau and have her ancestors hunted up. It transpired that the lady was really of noble lineage, but when she was shown the coat-of-arms which had belonged to her family centuries ago, she nearly fainted at the sight of the snakes and lizards that formed a prominent part of the crest. She declared that she hated "crawling things," and demanded a new one. The man of heralds tried to explain to her that the snakes and lizards were only symbols, but all to no effect, and he was finally obliged to make her a new coat-of-arms, in which frisking greyhounds took the place of the objectionable features.

It must, however, be admitted that the present system has its drawbacks as well as its conveniences, in that the owners of genuine crests are never safe in their possessions. If a neighbour admires the style and design, there seems to be nothing to prevent his having it copied, with, perhaps, a very small difference as regards details. It is said that an English diplomat, who some years ago resided in America, ordered from a Washington manufacturer a new brougham, with the instruction that on the panels should be painted his coat-of-arms. A few weeks later, on visiting the carriage shop, he found that several new turn-outs were standing about, emblazoned in the same way as the one he ordered. He thought, perhaps, the manufacturer was intending to make him a present.

" Are these all mine ? " he asked.

" Oh, no ! " answered the manufacturer. " Some of my customers so much admired the picture on your brougham that they decided to have it copied on their own carriages. Rather a compliment to your taste, I take ! " This story, however, is given more credence in England than in the United States.

I have found that none of the pedigree " shops " are entirely patronised by Americans. Many of their customers are to be found among the English middle classes. Snobs are not indigenous to republics. They are quite as numerous in monarchies.

There are certain people who do not care to patronise the " shops," preferring rather to carry on their transactions privately. It is mostly in this way that those persons who have a family backing and no money are enabled to meet others who have the money but no backing, and so they make a fair exchange, which is no robbery.

Since my investigation into this matter, I have begun to have a strangely suspicious feeling about some of my personal acquaintances, who, it has often occurred to me, talk more than is really necessary concerning their noble or gentle descent. I have even grown cynical as regards the thorough-bredness of my black poodle, whom I had hitherto looked upon as being descended from a long line of patrician Parisians. Now, whenever I notice him attempting to show any superiority over the unkempt mongrel that he passes on the street, I push back the fringe that hangs about his face and looking him in the eyes, say, "Dear old doggie! you must not be vain because of your supposed high-born condition, for I have discovered that there are PEDIGREES FOR ALL."

SWEEPING A CROSSING.

———◆◇◆———

"SPARE a copper! Spare a copper!" Every Londoner knows the hackneyed phrase. Walking one day from Oxford Circus to Charing Cross, I heard it fourteen times. "Help a poor chap!" "Pity an old sweep!" These were the variations which occasionally broke the monotony of the appeal. Into each outstretched hand I dropped a copper, while fourteen separate and distinct blessings were called down upon my head. When I reached the Strand I found I had distributed just twelve pence and a halfpenny, and I could have taken a hansom for a shilling! It was easy for me to understand why so many pedestrians were obliged to shake their heads at the importunities of the sweeps. It would be much cheaper to ride than to walk if one should hand to each sweep a penny or even a halfpenny, and cabs would be a matter of economy. Only the rich can afford to walk and be generous—or shall I say just? For, to my mind, it is a question whether people have a right to keep their boots clean on a muddy day without paying the man who makes it possible for them to walk dryshod across the street. I hold that the sweep is not a beggar, but a man of business, however humble his line of operations may be. When I walk over his cleanly-swept pathway with unsullied

J

skirts and boots I give him a penny as payment for value received, and in such cases a penny spent is two or three shillings saved in cleaners' bills.

The sweep is not only a man of business, he is often something of an artist. He has developed cross-sweeping into one of the fine arts, and no one can but admire the geometrical symmetry of his work. The straight lines stretching from corner to corner, the circles and right-angled triangles which he traces along the principal thoroughfares, often transform an ugly crossing into a thing of beauty. I have often wondered that some of the more skilful do not use their talents in a more remunerative profession, although wonderful tales have been told of members of the craft who have grown wealthy with plying the broom for a quarter of a century. Strange stories of men who swept crossings on week-days and rode in private broughams on Sundays are floating about London. A particularly interesting legend is that of an old man who for many years swept a crossing in the neighbourhood of Maryle-bone Road. He himself lived in cheap West-End lodgings, but his family had their country house, and fared sumptuously. Two or three times a year he visited them and made an impression on his neighbours with his always up-to-date method of dressing. His frock-coat and top-hat were of the latest make and fashion. When he died there were several thousand pounds to his credit in the bank. Among the ranks of crossing-sweeps the story will doubtless be handed down from father to son as an example of what an ambitious sweep may do if he will.

With an ever-inquiring mind that leads me often-
times into the amateur detective service in order to
get at the bottom of things, the idea of playing the
rôle of a crossing-sweep came to me as a matter of
course. I would thus have an opportunity to find
out if it were really true, as some people assert, that
hundreds of London sweeps are growing opulent at
the expense of poor but kind-hearted pedestrians.

With this in mind, I stopped to interview an old
woman who for the past several years has kept her
position on Portland Place, in the vicinity of the
Langham Hotel. I first took the precaution to give
her a goodly number of pennies ere I proceeded to
draw her out on the merits and demerits of her
chosen calling. She smiled propitiously, and then
I asked if I might hire her crossing for two hours
in the afternoon at the rate of a shilling an hour.
I had expected she would reply "Yes, lady. Thank
you, lady," and hand me over her broom and stool
without further parleying, but, to my astonishment,
she eyed me suspiciously and demanded sternly,
"What's yer motive?" I could not reply to her as
I had recently done to a London editor, who, when I
had proposed to him a subject for a sensational story,
put to me the same question. Then I had answered
candidly, "Why, to get copy, of course." I could not
thus take the old woman into my confidence.

"What difference can it make about my motive
so long as you get your money?" I asked. "See,
you may have it in advance," and I held the shining
coins temptingly before her.

She shook her head.

"I wants to know yer motive. Ye looks a fine

J 2

lady, but ye might be wantin' to take the bread out of my mouth!"

And so it was true that there were tricks in all trades, street-sweeping included! How, indeed, was she to know that I was not a would-be member of her craft passing myself off for a benevolent lady? Might I not have a deep-laid scheme to hire her stand for a couple of hours, and then "do" her out of her means of livelihood for the rest of her days?

"How much money did you take in yesterday?" I asked.

"Only ninepence, lady, enough to buy sugar and tea and bread, and the landlord was askin' me for the rent," she answered in a whining voice.

"Was that a good day's earnings?"

"Yes, lady; but sometimes I takes a shillin' or one and tuppence."

"Did you ever get two shillings in a day?"

"No, lady, never."

"Then why not take the money and let me have the crossing from three to five o'clock? Whatever pennies I receive I'll give you to-morrow morning."

My words were smooth and my tones seductive, but all to no avail.

"No, my lady. It do look queer, and I wouldn't let ye have it for no amount. Ye can't get a crossing from anybody unless ye tells more about yerself."

She picked up her broom and began wielding it excitedly over the pavement. Dismissed thus unceremoniously, I decided to go out sweeping on my own account, and commence operations wherever I could. An hour later I emerged from my area gate arrayed in the most suitable garments I could find about the house. Underneath my bodice, for warmth and inspiration, I wrapped about me a copy of the *Times*. I wore the black serge dress that had done duty a few months previous, when I held the responsible position of parlourmaid in Kensington, an old light coat, not of the newest cut, and a black cashmere shawl folded into a tippet for my neck. My head-covering was an old felt hat which had the appearance of having been through violent spasms and contortions. In order to disguise myself as much as possible until I could get out of my own neighbourhood, I had drawn a thick black veil over my face. Bearing in mind the story I had heard of the wealthy sweep of Marylebone Road, I wended my way towards the goal of his wondrous success. I hurried along Harley Street and turned off into the Marylebone Road, dragging my newly-purchased brushwood broom after me. My costume was not quite the orthodox thing for a sweep. The white jacket must have looked somewhat peculiar and out of place. What wonder that the butcher and baker boys hooted me as I passed at a rapid gait! "See the dandy sweep! Has yer got a licence, missus?" one of them called after me. No, I had not a licence; but I knew there were many other sweeps who also did not possess that important document, and I did not falter. A little fox-terrier, out for his morning constitutional, sniffed scornfully and barked ferociously at my heels, and such incidents tended only to quicken my pace.

At last I found a crossing over which there seemed to be no presiding genius, but I no sooner commenced operations than an angry-looking individual

"MY COSTUME WAS NOT QUITE ORTHODOX."

(*From a Photograph by the London Stereoscopic Company.*)

appeared, broom in hand, and shook it in my face. "Hi, there! what ye doing with my pitch? Ye'd better move on." As I did not know just what was the etiquette in vogue between members of the sweep brigade, I concluded it better to move on, and proceeded to Baker Street Station.

Many people were passing to and fro, and I thought it might be well to make a pathway of my own, a brand new one that no one could claim. I plied my broom most vigorously right and left, and did my best to clear a footroad across the mud for the patrons of the Underground Railway. In spite of my efforts, my work showed amateurishness. The style of broom I had chosen was an awkward one for me to handle, and for a while I only succeeded in spattering mud about. After great trouble and perseverance I made a path which looked as if a snake had wriggled across the road, and left a scalloped track behind him. When I stepped back upon the pavement to view my handiwork I felt that I had really earned a few pennies, for the route I had made was useful and ornamental as well.

The railway passengers began to cross over, but I did not hold out my hand for coppers, neither did I importune any one. I had determined to stand on all the dignity I had left, feeling that the labourer was worthy of his hire. People walked on my crossing, but nobody offered me payment. They took particular pains to keep themselves in the path, even in its most waggly parts. I began to despise them, and in my heart I called them paupers, to patronise my crossing and not be willing to pay for the privilege. They had no more right to take advantage of the track I had prepared than they had to go into a restaurant and eat a dinner for which they refused to pay. I felt that they were the beggars, not I. In my opinion, there was but one alternative for the person who was unwilling or unable to pay, and that was to go round on the outside through the mud. There was only one man who seemed to give the matter a thought. He put his hand into his pocket and pulled out a penny, then put it back again. He had probably expected to contribute a halfpenny, and found that he had not that coin in his possession.

In an hour I had become disgusted with the Baker Street Station neighbourhood, and I had grave doubts concerning the truthfulness of the wealthy sweep story. I could see no chance of riding in broughams or keeping country houses if I stuck to cross-sweeping in that vicinity, so I pulled my shawl about me, trying as best I could to cover up my white coat, and dragged my broom to Regent Street. I attracted little attention as I walked from Oxford Circus to Piccadilly. It was about one o'clock and many of the crossings were deserted. The sweeps were perhaps taking lunch. No one presided over the Vigo Street crossing, and I took up my stand there. But I did not attempt to sweep, thinking that, if the owner of the crossing suddenly made his appearance, I could deny any accusations he might make against my honesty by saying that I had simply stopped to rest a bit.

As I leaned on my broom I became intensely interested in the people who passed me. It was gloomy, muddy, and wet, and I took it for granted that those who walked on such a day walked because they could not afford to ride. A woman journalist of some fame but small fortune went by, clasping an envelope, which from its size and appearance I felt quite positive must contain manuscript. I did not ask her for a copper, for I was somehow under the impression that she was carrying her copy to Fleet Street because she had no stamps to send it by post.

"Belong here?" asked a man, sidling up to me. I recognised him as a sweep from across the way.

"Oh, no, I'm only resting," I answered wearily.

"It's hard times," he continued with an attempt at being sociable. "I've only took in tuppence to-day, but I've done some big splashing on the rest of 'em."

"Splashing! What for?" I asked.

"Well, ye must be a new un if ye don't know that trick! When I asks a man or a woman for a copper and they doesn't give it, I just splashes 'em; that's all."

What a pity I had not heard that before I took my stand near Baker Street Station!

The sweep went back to his stand, and I continued to view the procession of bedrabbled humanity that passed me. "Poor girl!" I heard someone say in pitying tones, and, looking up, I saw a much-painted and powdered, gaudily-dressed woman near me. "Take this," and she thrust a threepenny-bit into my hand. I managed to stammer out "Thank-you" as she sauntered on. It needed not a second look to tell me the class to which she belonged. Society, the pulpit, and the press number her among the "fallen." I have since been told that it is from these women that crossing-sweeps obtain most of their pennies.

About two o'clock the rain began to fall, and, as I

was not provided with an umbrella, I feared that a prolonged experiment in the street-sweeping line might unfit me for future explorations in various directions, so I turned my face homewards, with only the threepenny-bit as the result of my morning's work.

I have since taken the trouble to interview between twenty and thirty sweeps on the subject of taking out licences. I find that the majority of them do not approve of the licence system, which asks them to invest five shillings before they commence business. The matter of the licence is often neglected—perhaps I should say forgotten—till a policeman or other official gives them a gentle reminder.

I have also attempted to inspire them with a sense of the dignity of their calling, and have found it rather a difficult task, although they all agree with me that people who patronise their crossings should pay for it. Some of them have confidentially admitted that the stories of suffering wives, and children down with the measles or scarlet-fever, are invented to reach the sympathies of the public ; but they justify themselves in the belief that they are doing evil that good may come, and that what pennies they receive are given in charity. I have recommended to them that they get some sort of halfpenny-in-the-slot machine and place it in such a position that passers-by must see it and feel it incumbent upon them to contribute a halfpenny.

I am sure that such an arrangement would serve the purpose much better than the present method of collecting their dues.

A DAY WITH THE FLOWER-GIRLS.

'VIOLETS, sweet violets! A penny a bunch!" From ten o'clock in the morning until the first hour of midnight this cry of the flower-sellers may be heard in the London streets. It usually issues from female throats, although occasionally the clamour is reinforced by a masculine voice, which, however, could scarcely be more unpleasant or less musical than the voices of the women ; for they are not a prepossessing set of women in any respect, these London retailers of Flora's treasures. Dirty, coarse-featured, harsh-spoken, with draggled skirts, ragged shawls and befeathered hats of the latest coster style, they seem ill-suited to be the vendors of velvety violets and waxen lilies. Travellers who have seen the Continental flower-girls in their bright, picturesque costumes that, in point of attractiveness, vie with the blossoms they offer to passers-by, cannot help but wish that the street-corners and circuses of gloomy London might also be thus enlivened. In accordance with the law of the eternal fitness of things, it is proper enough that those who brush our streets and sweep our chimneys should be muddy and grimy, but there is something incongruous in the sight of an unkempt, vicious-looking female, handling and selling beautiful flowers, while in shrill, clarion tones she tells us that she has " Lubly biolets, English

biolets. No furrin biolets without a smell, is these,
mum!" I am convinced that smiles and fame and
a fortune await the dainty dealer in *boutonnières*, who,
attractive herself, and attractively attired, will take
her stand for a few weeks at Oxford, Piccadilly, or
Ludgate Circus.

To discover something of the ins and outs and
the ups and downs of flower-selling, and to investigate into the ways of living and the aims and
ambitions of the London flower-girls, I spent a
Saturday in February among them. Had my object
been the establishment of a new dynasty of flower-
sellers, I should only too gladly have attired myself
after the manner of the Italian girls, and have turned
into a living London reality my notion of the ideal
flower-girl. But under the circumstances I thought
it better to leave the introduction of the new order
to some other daring spirit, while taking for myself
the much more difficult and unpleasant task of
searching after the merits and demerits of the
present race.

I chose Saturday for my exploit, thinking that
matinée afternoon must naturally be the harvest-
time of the week. At eight o'clock in the morning,
arrayed in black dress, black shawl, and brown straw
hat trimmed with pink roses, I visited the Covent
Garden Flower Market to make my purchases at
wholesale rates. Having, in the privacy of my own
house, tried the effect of a great, heavy, cumbersome
basket, such as is commonly used, dangling from
my neck, I decided that it was far too ugly and
weighty for me to handle; so I carried in its stead
a light round basket, and tied it about my neck with

a ribbon. When I arrived, the proprietors of the various stalls in the market were doing a thriving business. Scores of coster-women, with the appearance of having been neither washed nor combed since they got out of bed, were rushing about from stall to stall, bent on discovering where they could buy the most flowers for the least money. "How much?" they would ask, snatching a cluster of lilies or hyacinths from a box and holding it in the face of the dealer. On being told the price, their faces would contort into a fiendish scowl, as they answered, "Go 'long! What yer sayin'? Don't ye want me to make no pruffit?"

The flower market usually closes shortly after nine o'clock, and it is between eight and nine—in order to have their wares as fresh as possible—that the girls make their daily purchases. I followed several of them about the place while they were in pursuit of their bargains. Their manners and language were something of a revelation to me. I had expected to find them coarse and rough, but I was not prepared for such obscene and profane talk as I heard. With many, all semblance of womanly modesty seemed to be a thing of the long-gone past. They swore at each other and coquetted with the market men. While holding out their aprons to receive the flowers for which they had paid, they would slyly pass their hands into boxes in their vicinity and take possession of many a bunch for which they had not paid. I afterwards learned that this habit of petty thievery among them is one of their greatest sources of profit, for the sales of flowers thus obtained are, of course, all gain.

On the morning in question violets sold wholesale at the rate of sixpence and eightpence a dozen
bunches ; lilies of the valley were tenpence a dozen
sprays.

When the girls had completed their purchases,
some of those who lived near went home to arrange
their baskets, while others sat down on stones and
stools outside the market, and proceeded to get
ready for the day's work. I became intensely
interested in watching them assort their flowers.
In the majority of cases I noticed that from two
market bunches they very deftly and quickly manufactured three. Then sticks and strings were brought
into requisition, and in less than half an hour all
was in readiness. I approached one of these girls
in a meek, bashful way, and asked her if she would
show me how to arrange my basket. Her refusal
to help me was particularly emphatic—so much so
that I thought it discreet to leave her—for in the
most pronounced Cockney she informed me that I
had best move on and away, else she would give
me a "jab in the eye." I held no further converse
with her, feeling that, although under ordinary circumstances I was capable of holding my own in a
war of words, I was more than likely to come out
only second best in a fist encounter.

In a group just outside the market were three
generations of flower-sellers. The oldest woman
was about fifty years of age. Her daughter and
granddaughter stood near sorting flowers, and afterwards each took her way to different parts of
London. I have been told that the business of
flower-selling is hereditary, and that nearly all of

the London flower-girls have, or had, mothers, grandmothers, and even great-grandmothers, engaged in the same line. The trade is handed down from mother to daughter, and the girls have often given to them a little hoard of money laid aside by their ancestors.

After I had purchased two dozen bunches of violets at eightpence a dozen, two clusters of lilies at tenpence each, and a bundle of moss for a penny, I obtained the permission of a woman in the market to sit down on an up-turned basket in her stall and complete the arrangement of my outfit for the day. My ideas on this subject had been more theoretical than practical; for, with all my preparations for making an artistic-looking basket, I had neglected to provide myself with a very important item— a shingle, with small holes, in which to place my flowers, to make them stand upright. The market-woman came to my assistance with a bit of paste-board, and with my pocket-knife I bored holes the proper size to hold the stems of my bunches. After the violets were fitted in, I divided the lilies into clusters of three sprays each and put them in odd corners. Then between the rows of violets I sprinkled the green moss. Once finished, my basket was certainly a dainty-looking affair, and I felt no doubt that I should carry on a good trade.

As I left Covent Garden, and hurried along the Strand, I think I must have had the air of a rather superior sort of flower-girl, for several persons eyed me rather curiously. When, at last, having reached Piccadilly Circus and taken my stand under a lamp-post, I opened my mouth to inform the passers-by that I had "Violets, sweet violets, at a penny a bunch," I started at the sound of my own voice.

I had not been there many minutes before I heard someone say, "Oh, what a beautiful basket!"

Turning to the speaker, I picked out one of the bunches and repeated the price of my wares. The admirer of my basket was a young lady accompanied by a gentleman, who immediately purchased one bunch of lilies and two of violets.

He looked at me kindly and said, "Selling many flowers to-day?"

"Not yet," I answered; "I'm just out. This is my first day in business."

The young lady smiled encouragingly, and said, "You'll surely sell a good many. You look so nice and neat, and your basket is so pretty!"

As the gentleman was handing me fivepence, his fair companion suggested that he give me an extra penny for luck, so from that deal I received sixpence.

My artistic-looking basket attracted many customers who, I felt sure, would not otherwise have thought of buying flowers.

"My, what a fine spread you have!" observed a young man to whom I sold a *boutonnière*.

In a little cushion at the side I carried some pins, so I fastened the violets on his coat-lapel, and he, too, smiled benignly upon me and gave me twopence instead of a penny.

Noticing a grey-haired, benevolent-looking lady standing at a shop window, and thinking she might be a possible customer, I went towards her.

"Violets, lady, violets?" I asked, looking at her in a pitifully appealing way.

"I FELT MEEK AND LOWLY."

(From a Photograph by the London Stereoscopic Company.)

K

"No, no, child," she replied, almost savagely; and, after that repulse, I made no further advances to benevolent-looking ladies. It did not take me long to discover that the men were my best customers, and that those accompanied by ladies were always the most generous. Were I a permanent flower-girl, I should devote my attention almost exclusively to such men. He would be a man of particularly stony heart who could refuse to buy a bouquet after the fair creature at his side had said—"Oh, what beautiful violets! How artistically they are arranged!"

Two or three times I left my post and wandered along the middle of the sidewalk, where I did quite a flourishing business.

"Get out of this! Can't ye see ye block the way?" said a policeman, taking me by the shoulders and pushing me towards the edge of the walk.

It was wonderful what that change of costume had done for me! With the clothes I had donned, and the basket I carried, I seemed to have put on a new character and a different temperament. That day I felt like a flower-girl—not, certainly, like my coarse-voiced associates who were gathered across the way about the fountain, but like a meek and lowly dealer in blossoms, with a strange sort of impression that, in some way, my daily bread depended on my selling those flowers.

Had I been my natural self when that policeman spoke to me, Piccadilly Circus would have been enlivened by a combat between an officer of the law and an angry maiden; but I was not myself—I was somebody else—and I received his rebuke mildly as a lamb, and returned to my position under the lamp-post.

As *matinée* time came on, my flowers sold even more readily, and my basket was soon more than half empty. Just then I noticed one of the flower-girls from the fountain coming over towards me. When she reached my stand she shook her fist angrily at me.

"Yer hundersellin' us! What d'yer mean by it?" she demanded.

"Why, what have I done to you?" I asked, wonderingly.

"Yer sellin' violets for a penny a bunch the same as we's selling for tuppence. Wait till I catch ye! A laidy just said we wus cheatin' her."

In the short time I had sold flowers I had become a marvel of meekness and gentleness, and I did not stop to argue the point out with her. "Violets, sweet violets, a penny a bunch!" I sang out as a dashing young man passed me, and my discomfited opponent left me, muttering threats of dreadful vengeance to be visited upon me in future.

"Violets, sir?" I said to a kind-looking, red-whiskered man. He shook his head, whereupon I gave him a sorrowful, melancholy look. The man turned back. "I think I'll have a couple of bunches," he said, fumbling in his pocket for change. My look of woe-begoneness had its effect. While I stood there, three men of clerical dress and mien passed me, but they did not purchase violets.

"Yes, we must take a bunch to Auntie," I heard someone say, and then, "Why, she's got just enough for us."

"How much?" asked a pretty little boy in a sailor suit, taking up a bunch of lilies.

K 2

" Threepence," I answered.

The important-looking man who held the little boy's hand gave me a sixpence for the lilies and two bunches of violets.

"Keep the change," said he; "now you're sold out, and you'll have to fill your basket again."

So many people spoke kindly to me that afternoon that I began to think that the world was not so hard, after all, even for a flower-girl.

It was four o'clock, and my basket was empty. I tried to refill it by getting flowers from some of my companions in trade, but they demanded such exorbitant prices for their wares that I decided to return to Covent Garden and buy another dozen bunches from the general dealers there. I could not procure them as cheaply as I had done in the morning, and was obliged to pay the regular price, a penny a bunch. However, they were large, and I thought ought to retail for twopence a bunch.

When I passed again through the Strand people were going home from the *matinées*, and I stopped in front of two of the theatres hoping to make some sales. It was a bad time. Those who wanted flowers had been supplied before going to the theatre, and I did not sell any.

A poorly-clad little girl of eleven or twelve years old, carrying a few sprays of drooping hyacinths, stopped me with " How much for violets, missus? "

" Twopence a bunch," I answered.

" Make 'em cheaper," she pleaded; " that's all I can sell 'em for."

Then I realised that she was one of my kind, and when I knew this mite of humanity was in the 'profession," I sold her three bunches for twopence, the price of one. What was my loss was her gain. If she sold them, she made fourpence on the bargain.

I returned to Piccadilly Circus with nine bunches of violets.

"I'll take a bunch," said a young woman, handing me a penny."

"Twopence, please, lady," I answered sadly, but firmly. I was becoming a thorough business woman, and was determined to sell my goods at a profit or not sell them at all. The young woman walked away without buying. It grew darker and colder, and I still had nine bunches of violets to dispose of. My bare hands were getting purple, and I was hungry, having had no luncheon. The Circus began to get deserted, so I decided to move my stand of operations westward. Walking leisurely towards Oxford Circus, I repeated, at stated intervals, my very subdued cry of "Violets! violets! twopence a bunch!" but there seemed to be no magic in the words. No buyers came to my call. Half-way between the Circuses a swagger-looking man rushed past me, threw two pennies into my basket, refused to take the flowers I held out to him, and left me bewildered, wondering whether he was a sinner trying to ease his conscience by doing a good deed in a wicked world, a lunatic, or a philanthropist. I was sorry he did not take his due, for I was as anxious to dispose of my flowers as to take in money. I wanted to go home, but I had a certain pride which forbade my returning home with such a quantity of unsold goods on my hands.

At six o'clock I was still standing at a corner of Oxford Circus, when I suddenly remembered that a literary acquaintance of mine (a well-known author), who was a recent convert to the "newer journalism," had a dinner-party on that evening, and it occurred to me that my violets would make very appropriate favours for his guests. My tired feet bore me in the direction of Regent's Park, where, after sundry explanations of myself and my business, I induced the great man to purchase my violets. He very generously gave me two shillings for the lot, an advance of fourpence on the price asked. Thus it was that the bread I cast upon the waters when I sold the little flower-girl three bunches for twopence' brought me immediate results.

Returning home, I settled up my day-book, and this is how the page stood :—

PAID OUT.

					s.	d.
2 Dozen violets at 8d.	...	...	...		1	4
1 Dozen violets at 1s.	...	...	...		1	0
2 Clusters lilies at 10d.	...	...	...		1	8
1 Bundle moss	...	...	...	...	0	1
					4	1

TOOK IN.

					s.	d.
24 Sprays lilies at 1d.	...	...	...		2	0
1 Dozen violets at 2d.	...	...	...		2	0
2 Dozen violets at 1d.	...	...	...		2	0
Had given me	...	...	...	...	0	5
					6	5
Profit	...	...	...	...	...	2	4

When my accounts were settled, I was not over-

whelmed with the amount of my profits. Two shillings
and fourpence a day was not a large wage, to be
sure! However, I took into consideration the fact
that it was my first day, that I was new to the
business, and I felt that, if I continued to work at
the trade, I might reasonably expect to sell more
flowers and make greater profits. Perhaps by selling
flowers in the evening, as well as during the day, I
might be able to make three shillings a day after I
got fairly started, but that was as high as my ambition allowed me to soar. That would only be
eighteen shillings a week. Yet I have been told
that the majority of the London flower-girls usually
take in more than twice, and sometimes three times,
that amount of money during the week, and I am
in a quandary as to how the thing is done.

But there are certain tricks of the trade, such as
the dividing of the market bunches, taking possession of more flowers than they pay for, selling ten
bunches for a dozen, and other similar schemes.

Although I have not, perhaps, spent as much
time in investigating into the condition of the
flower-girls as some may think necessary before
passing an opinion, I am bound to say that, from
what I have seen and learned of them, I cannot look
upon them as a particularly deserving class of individuals. They are unprepossessing in appearance, loud
and rude in their manners, and I am inclined to think
that the morals of many of them would not bear a
close scrutiny. Some charitable ladies who have
attempted to work among them say that they are a
difficult class to reach, and that sympathy and kindness are usually wasted upon them. Not having

tried the work of reformation, I am not able to speak authoritatively on that point ; and I should not care to go as a missionary amongst them. They impress me as being of a too combative disposition to make pleasant companions.

AMONG THE LAUNDRY-GIRLS.

CHAPTER I.

WHY AND HOW I BECAME ONE OF THEM.

THE laundry question is like the domestic servant problem. It interests everyone in all classes of society. If it is true that "civilised man cannot live without cooks," it is equally true that he cannot do without a laundress. Indeed, a man's happiness is to a greater degree dependent upon his laundress than his cook. Nothing can so quickly transform a kind, thoughtful, and good-tempered man into a frightful specimen of total depravity as a badly-ironed shirt-front or a limply-starched collar. Even men of the most angelic dispositions and piously inclined have been known to lapse into profanity over just such trifles. On second thought, "trifles" is not the word I should have used, for I agree that, of all the deplorable-looking objects in the world, a man not properly "done up" is the worst. A man's personal appearance depends quite as much upon his shirt-fronts and collars and cuffs as a woman's good looks depend upon the way she arranges her hair.

Despite the fact that I live in the days of the "new womanhood," which demands stiff shirts, high collars, neckties, and waistcoats as proofs of complete "emancipation," I still hold to the belief that boiled shirts are, or should be, a man's exclusive property, and I can readily understand his objection to the "new woman" who, in her fierce clamour for what she calls her "rights," will not stop to consider the wrongs she is inflicting on the opposite sex, and, not content with having, in some professions, deprived man of his means of livelihood, would now take away from him his very clothes.

There is one thing in connection with the subject of laundry work that I have never been able to understand, and that is the rooted objection that most men have to paying their washerwomen. One would think that, dependent as they are upon these women for half their life's happiness, they would, if they could, pay them promptly and without protest. Why men always object to paying laundry bills is something beyond my comprehension. Bachelors in good standing, socially and financially, who are noted for discharging every other obligation, even to their tailors, will let the poor laundress wait for weeks, months, and sometimes years, and then allow her to sue them for her long-accumulated bill. They seem to do these things on general principles. It was but a few weeks ago that the papers reported the case of a nobleman who, out of pure contrariness, refused for three years to pay his laundry bill, although perfectly able to do so; and it was only after he was brought into court and the judge had remonstrated with him, giving him the choice of either paying up or going to gaol, that he would even consider the matter seriously. Laundresses say that men of means give them more trouble than any other customers; and proprietors of lodging-houses and hotels assert that well-to-do men, who can always be relied upon to pay for their board and apartments when due, will each week pin their laundry accounts upon the wall, until in time the pattern of the wall-paper is almost hidden from sight by these unreceipted bills. It is easy enough to understand why the man in the state of "broke" allows such things to happen ; but why gentlemen of means should be so prejudiced is a puzzle that I doubt if even they themselves would be able to solve.

About once in a decade the public is agitated over some new or old phase of the laundry question. A few years ago the whole of the United States was nearly frightened out of existence over the subject. Somebody (I believe it was *not* a newspaper reporter) one day took his linen to a Chinese laundry, and saw a Chinaman in the other end of the room with a white scar on his face. "White spots are symbols of leprosy," thought he, and then he went to talk the matter over with a medical man, who immediately got out his books on the subject. In a week the papers had taken the matter up, and John Chinaman was in a fair way to lose all his customers. Everybody talked about the dangers of leprosy. People who lived in hotels, flats, or boarding-houses, where washing must be sent out, were thrown into violent hysterics when told by the doctors that many of the Chinese laundrymen were lepers, and that the disease could be communicated by means of clean linen, until finally America became the land of the great unwashed. The baskets of soiled linen got full to overflowing, because people were afraid to send them to the laundries, while the shops, especially men's furnishing houses, carried on a thriving trade. Ladies living in hotels, where conspicuous among the rules of the house was the legend, "No Washing Allowed in the Rooms," locked and barred their bedroom doors, and washed handkerchiefs and stockings in the wash-bowl or bath-tub, then hung them on the bed-posts and chair-backs to dry, and with the solitary iron they had surreptitiously purchased, smoothed the clothes out on the floor.

At that particular time the politician took advantage of the panic to announce from legislative halls and lecture platforms that "the Chinese must go," and very few there were who ventured to contradict him. After a while the tumult subsided, and it was succeeded by the "typhus scare" and the "cholera scare."

We make a speciality of "scares" in the United States. Sometimes we are able to run two or three at once, but we are never without one. Our peculiar temperament and the variable climate demand this sort of excitement, and when one "scare" is past, and another takes its place, we are neither better nor worse off than we were before.

I do not suppose that I should ever again have thought of the "laundry scare" had I not gone to reside in lodgings for a time, and so put on my own responsibility as regarded the choice of a laundress. Even then I did not trouble myself much about it, except to tell the housemaid to get me a laundress, and she provided me with the person who did the washing for the other lodgers. For a few weeks all went on well enough, until I one day picked up a medical paper and read an article about "Infection from Laundries," in which the writer told terrible tales of how inoffensive people, especially

those living in lodgings, suddenly found themselves
stricken down with smallpox, scarlet-fever, or diph-
theria, all because their clothes were washed under
unsanitary conditions. The writer warned his readers
against sending their linen to laundries consisting
of but one room, which served not only for wash-
house and drying-grounds, but bedroom, sitting-
room, kitchen, and goat-stable as well. When I
came to the part which advised everybody to find
out for himself and herself just how and where their
clothes were washed, it dawned upon me that, in
failing to make the acquaintance of my own laundress, I had been guilty of a crime against myself
and society at large. What if I should get smallpox
or scarlet-fever, all because of my neglect of this
matter!

I rang the bell for the housemaid. Again and
again I turned the handle, until peal after peal re-
sounded through the house.

"Martha, who washes my clothes?" I demanded,
when at the end of half an hour's ringing, she made
her appearance.

"I think her name is Mrs. Johnstone, miss,"
answered Martha, looking at me in a strangely suspicious way; and then she added, "Did she lose
anything last week?"

"Do you mean to say that you are not sure of
the woman's name?" I asked, paying no attention
to her solicitude in regard to the number of "pieces"
that had been returned.

"I'm quite sure it's Johnstone," she answered
again, this time with more decision.

"What is her address?"

" I can't tell you at all, miss."

" That's strange. I must know where **she** lives. I want to call on her."

Then Martha suggested that the landlady would probably know, so she went down-stairs and returned with the information that Mrs. Johnstone lived " somewhere near 'Ammersmith," but nobody knew just where.

It was Tuesday, and the clothes would not be returned until Saturday, and there seemed to be no way of obtaining the address before that time. I blamed the washerwoman for not having yet sent me a bill with her name and address at the top, and I despised the landlady and all her lodgers because of their stupidity. To discover the whereabouts of a Mrs. Johnstone who lived somewhere near Hammersmith looked like a feat far beyond my powers of accomplishment, but that medical paper had wrought my nerves up to such a state that I could neither eat nor write nor sleep until I had at least made an attempt to find her.

I went to the post-office and consulted that part of the " Directory " given up to the J's, and the multitude of Mrs. Johnstones who lived somewhere near Hammersmith and took in washing threatened to deprive me of my reason. Visions of a horrible hovel, with babies and goats and chickens galore, and a sickly-looking woman washing my best handkerchiefs in poverty, hunger, and dirt, rose continually before me, and would not be dispelled. Yet I could spare neither the time nor the money that the finding of Mrs. Johnstone would involve. What little reason I had left told me that the only thing I could do

was to wait till Saturday; so I gave Martha instructions to get the woman's full name and address
when she returned the clothes. Then I tried to
compose myself to write a paper on "The Duty of
Self-Control," but my thoughts were all of wash-tubs
and ironing-boards, and I decided that I ought to
know more about the laundry business than I did. I
began to think not only about small washerwomen,
but steam-laundries and laundry-girls, who, according
to common report, were the most wicked of their sex
in London. I had heard direful tales of the way they
pulled each other's hair, scratched one another's eyes
out, and insulted good people who tried to reform
them.

Having once got so far interested in the subject,
it was but natural that I should follow it up in the
only way that I could conceive of getting correct
information, and that was by becoming a laundry-
girl myself.

In order to get a situation, I answered all the
advertisements for "learners" that I could find in the
morning papers, and then I inserted an advertisement
on my own account :—

A YOUNG WOMAN wants a situation in a large
first-class Laundry, where she can learn the
business. No wages.

It was on that last clause that I most depended
for my answers, for I knew there were many people
who were waiting to secure something for nothing. I
was particularly careful in the wording of my advertisement, so that it should not in any way resemble
the one I had inserted when I sought a place in
domestic service. I determined that, in this instance,

I would not pose as an " educated and refined young woman." That sort of thing could not be tried again. The proprietor of a laundry would not know how to " place " such qualities.

While I waited for applicants for my services, which I had no doubt would be numerous, I busied myself in preparing for a week in a laundry. I got together a suit of clothes neither conspicuously unbecoming nor altogether too nice—a sort of medium between the coster and shop-girl style—in which I might apply for a place ; and I bought a black-and-white polka-dot blouse and apron for work in the laundry. The subject of references would not, I thought, be so troublesome as it had been when I was seeking a place as housemaid, but I arranged to have a reference given if it should be required. I feared that my greatest difficulty would be my American accent, which for the past three months I had tried to lose (for professional purposes only). But it was still quite as pronounced as on the day I arrived in London, and was continually getting me into trouble when I endeavoured to pass for somebody else. Yet now I trusted to Providence that I would not be called upon to account for it when I applied for a situation in a laundry, because, once asked if I were an American, it was always necessary for me to depart from strict veracity in order to explain how I happened to be in London.

Much to my disappointment, I received no answers on the next day nor the day following, and my faith in advertising as a means of obtaining anything and everything began to waver. At the end of the week one lone letter was handed to me. It was

from the Y—— and Z—— Sanitary Laundry in an
East London suburb, and in it I was informed that in
this laundry there was just such a place as I had
advertised for, and I was asked to call on Saturday morning. I had also another appointment at
ten o'clock on Saturday with the only person who
had answered one of the many letters I had written
applying for a place. This was in the neighbourhood
of Streatham, and I went there first.

Mrs. S——, the "proprietress" of the place, opened
the door. From a height of six feet and a breadth of
little less, she looked at me in amazement when I
told her I was "Lizzie Barnes," who had written to
her for a place as "learner." It was the same old
story, "too little!" I assured her that, though small,
my strength was little short of that possessed by
Samson, and I reiterated the statement I had made
in my letter to her that I could "iron good."

The result was that in half an hour Mrs. S——
concluded to give me a trial, not only at the ironing-
board, but in what she called the "washus." She
made no remarks about my American accent, neither
did she ask for references, and I concluded it would
be well for me to accept the situation, not knowing
whether it would be possible to secure another one.

While talking with Mrs. S——, it occurred to me
that the proprietors of the Y—— and Z—— Laundry
might not be so favourably impressed with my abilities
as a laundress, so I told her I would like to try the
place. She explained that her laundry (" landry " she
called it) was only a small one, where but six girls were
employed, and that all the work was done by hand.
The "washus" was in the basement of the house, but

L

the rest of the work was done in a red-brick building, which I could see in the rear of the house. From the windows I noticed several girls ironing, while in the yard a frowzy-haired young woman was taking down clothes from the line.

"Will you take me through the laundry?" I asked, curious to get a look at the girls with whom I expected to associate for the next week or longer.

"Oh, no, Saturday is such a busy day, I can't do that," she answered; and, plead as I would, I could not induce her to gratify my curiosity. But she was very sociable, offered me a glass of ale, and, when I refused it, said she thought I would have to take beer if I went into the laundry business. Then the question of "living in" came up. She was not particularly anxious that I should "live in," for, of course, that would necessitate her giving me my board; but to "live in" was a part of my plan, because all the girls lived there together, and Mrs. S——, remembering that, after all, I was not to receive any wages, and that a person of my size was not likely to have an enormous appetite, agreed to "put me up" with the other girls.

I had engaged to go on the next Tuesday, and was leaving the door, when I thought to ask if I should have a bed to myself. Mrs. S—— was quite surprised at the question, and explained that, as there was but one room with three beds, and as I would make the sixth girl, a bed to myself would be an impossibility. I decided that I would prefer to "live out" and board myself, and when I bade her good morning, it was arranged that I was to go to work the next Tuesday morning.

When I called at the Y—— and Z—— Sanitary
Laundry, I regretted my haste in engaging myself to
Mrs. S——. This laundry was worked by steam ;
there were about thirty girls employed, and I felt sure
that the experience I would gain there would be of
greater advantage to me. But Mrs. Morris, the wife
of the proprietor of the laundry, was by no means at
first inclined to take me, because I seemed to know
nothing about the business. However, I assured her,
as I had done Mrs. S——, that I could "iron good,"
which was to a certain extent true.

"You mean you know how to do plain ironing ? "
she asked.

"Yes. When I lived home, I did all the family
washing and ironing," I answered ; and even now
I wonder how I ever dared to say it.

Mrs. Morris looked at me rather sharply when
I told her of my abilities in the way of washing and
ironing.

"Where was that ? " she asked.

Then a nursery rhyme of my childhood days ran
quickly through my mind—

"Oh, what a tangled web we weave
When first we practise to deceive,"

but, nevertheless, I answered, " In Australia."

"I knew you couldn't be a Londoner. I thought
you talked something like an American, but I suppose the accent is about the same ? " said Mrs.
Morris.

"Yes ; I'm an Australian. I lived there with my
brother, but I came to London, and want to learn the
laundry business."

L 2

Why I declared myself an Australian I hardly knew. I only thought I must say I was from some place far away, as Mrs. Morris might ask me for more particular references than I was prepared to give. It was fortunate for me that she knew nothing more about Australia than I knew, so that no embarrassment followed, except that, as I looked across the room, one of the ironing-tables seemed suddenly covered with stars and stripes that somehow worked themselves into letters that spelt "TRAITOR!"

Try as I would, I did not succeed in inspiring Mrs. Morris with any sense of my capabilities, but she took me to her husband to ask him what he thought about it. He was also doubtful as to whether I was strong enough, but I begged so hard to be allowed to show what I could do, that he said, "Suppose we try her, as she don't want any wages," and I was engaged.

I was told to come in next Tuesday, at the same hour at which I had agreed to go to Mrs. S——. With two situations on hand, the work to commence at the same hour of the same day, it was clear I must give up one of them ; so I wrote to Mrs. S—— that I had decided not to take the place, as it would be too expensive to "live out" and not agreeable to "live in."

On Monday, having obtained Mrs. Johnstone's address, I inspected her laundry, and found it to be a very proper sort of establishment, with a good wash-house, clean ironing-room, and a little yard for drying clothes. But I did not send my clothes to her that week ; I thought I would prefer to have them go to the Y—— and Z—— Sanitary Laundry, where I

might have the novel experience of giving them my
personal attention, so I had them sent there, and on
Tuesday I was ready to commence my career as a
laundry-girl.

CHAPTER II.

AT WORK IN A "SANITARY LAUNDRY."

AN atmosphere thick with steam and the odour of
boiling soap-suds greeted me Tuesday morning, when
I arrived at the Y—— and Z—— Sanitary Laundry
to take my situation as a "learner." Ironing-machine,
wringer, and mangle were revolving at a rapid rate,
propelled by the large engine. Water was sputter-
ing from the boilers in which the clothes were being
washed ; a dozen girls and women were ironing,
others were starching, sprinkling, or folding clothes,
and a solitary water-soaked individual presided in
one corner over some wash-tubs, applying a scrub-
bing-brush to clothes that could not be put into
the machines. All the work was done in one immense room, floored over with cement, which was a
succession of hills and hollows, more dangerous in
aspect than any American pavement. One side of
the room was taken up with an ironing-machine and
ironing-tables, the other side with the engine, boilers,
wringer, mangle, and wash-tubs. A corner, in the
vicinity of the engine, was floored over with some
boards, and fitted up with crude-looking tables and
a half-dozen large boxes. It was called the "sorting-
room," and it was there that I was conducted by Mrs.

Morris when I had removed my coat and hat and donned my working costume. Between the door and the sorting corner there stretched a large body of

"A DOZEN GIRLS AND WOMEN WERE IRONING."

soapy water, several yards square, and in some places almost ankle-deep.

"Pick your skirts up," said Mrs. Morris, as she prepared to lead me across. I was on the point of asking for a boat and ferryman, when I saw her step into the water and walk bravely over ; so, acting on the principle that the employée was no better than the employer, I also walked across, and landed with wet feet. I supposed that, of course, there had been an accident, that one of the boilers had turned upside down ; but I was afterwards told that the pond was always there. It was let out from the washing-machines in which the linen was boiled, and allowed to flow about the place until it found its way to a small sewer underneath a board, where it sunk into the ground, and its place was taken by more water from the next boiler of clothes. Taking into consideration the fact that I was in a " sanitary " laundry, it was only natural that I should have been surprised that there were no pipes for the purpose of carrying off this water.

In the sorting-corner I was introduced to Miss Stebbins, the head packer and sorter, a position considered to be the most genteel in the business. It was there that I spent the first three days of my apprenticeship.

Until I was set to making figures with red cotton I had never thought of connecting needlework and laundry work. I had supposed my career as a needlewoman was ended when, just before I left Mrs. Allison's, I darned up the contents of the mending-basket; but darning was as nothing compared with the making of figures with red cotton. With constantly-pricked fingers and agitated temper, I tried my best to stitch into the linen the numbers that Miss Stebbins instructed me to make, and, after much perseverance, I succeeded in learning all the figures except 5 and 6. Those two I would never have learned to make had not Janie, one of the girls, come to my assistance.

Janie was a sort of general utility maid for everybody about the place. She was short and slightly lame, and one shoulder was somewhat lower than the other.

JANIE.

Her face had a strangely-combined expression of childhood and womanhood upon it. She had large, wandering blue eyes that looked glad and sad by turns; and her hair hung down her back, half-braided, half-loose, after the fashion of the young girls who live in the East-End. She was an illustration of perpetual motion. She rarely sat down, and seldom stood still. There was an indescribable something about her that made her seem oddly at variance with her surroundings. She looked as if she should have painted pictures or made music for the world, instead of living in and breathing an atmosphere of soap-suds.

It was towards the end of the second day, when I had been vainly endeavouring to embroider the figure 6 on the corner of a serviette, that Janie came over to the sorting corner and accosted me with—

"Hi'll 'elp you, Miss Barnes."

She took my thimble and needle, and her nimble fingers soon worked out not only one 6 but a dozen of them on a piece of calico she picked up from the floor. She did not sit down, and her feet kept up a rat-tat-tat on the boards while she gave me my lesson.

When five o'clock came, and the girls were allowed a half-hour for tea, Janie invited me over to the other side of the room to share the large pot of tea that she had made for herself and older sister, who was one of the ironers, and at the rate of five farthings a shirt was sometimes able to earn three-and-six a day— more money than any other woman in the laundry was capable of earning. She poured the tea from the rusted pot into a thick cup minus a handle, and ordered me to drink it quickly, so that she might also have her tea, for there were only two cups for the three persons. Never medicine was more difficult to swallow than Janie's tea. It tasted stale, and strong, and bitter, although quantities of queer-looking brown sugar had been put into it; but I drank it down heroically.

During this half-hour the ironing-boards were turned into tea-tables, and, as Mr. and Mrs. Morris had gone into the house, which adjoined the laundry, for their own tea, the workers had a few minutes for social intercourse. A dark-skinned, demure-looking girl sat on a box by the collar-machine, over which she presided during working hours, and read the *Church Missionary Intelligencer* and *Church Missionary Gleaner*, while she sipped her tea. Janie whispered to me that it was Annie Martin, who was very religious, and wanted to become a missionary, but, on account of a defective education, was unable to pass the examination that was required.

Janie's sister munched her bread-and-butter and read a penny novel at the same time; while Mrs. Bruckerstone, one of the older women, entertained the assemblage by giving a practical illustration of the difference between "piece-work" and "day-work." She showed how, in doing piece-work, where the number of articles ironed governed the amount of pay, the worker moved about briskly and eagerly. Then, in illustration of day-work, she picked up an apron, shook it out, smoothed it on the board, patted it down, and took her time over ironing it. During that half-hour I became acquainted with all the women in the place, and was surprised to find that they were not at all like the description I had always heard of laundry-girls. I heard no profanity, no bad language, and no quarrelling. With the exception of a few older women, most of them were girls between the ages of fifteen and twenty-five. However, Janie told me that the girls employed in the Y—— and Z—— Laundry were superior to those engaged in the surrounding laundries. It seems they did scratch, and fight, and swear in a laundry only a mile distant; but Mr. and Mrs. Morris made it a point to keep their place rather "select" as regarded the characters of their employées.

When Janie and I returned to the marking, she regaled me with an account of all the accidents to which girls working in steam laundries were liable, and this in no way added to my peace of mind. It appeared that boilers sometimes blew up, although they had never done so in the Y—— and Z—— Laundry; leather belts flew off the wheels and hit the bystander's eyes; fingers were mashed, and

sometimes clipped off, in working at the mangle
and wringer. Only recently one of the girls had
been taken away to the hospital, where she had been
obliged to have three of her fingers amputated,
because they had slipped into the rubber rollers of
the wringer. But Janie declared this affair was all
due to carelessness, as the girl was looking about and
talking, instead of attending to her work. One of
Janie's fingers, I noticed, was flattened, but it had not
been done at the laundry. She had been chopping
wood, and hit it with an axe.

"Hi'm always in the wars, Miss Barnes," said she.
"When Hi were a baiby, Hi were dropped on the
paivement, and the bruise went hinside instead of
hout. That's what maikes me laime."

"How did you get the scar on your forehead?" I
asked.

"Hi fell on the fender."

Poor little Janie! she really had been through
the wars. If there was any trouble with the
girls or the customers, she was always sent to
make it right. If anything got lost, she must hunt
until she found it, though having nothing to do with
the losing of it. If delinquent customers refused to
pay their bills, Janie was sent to make the collections,
and usually returned with the money. A few days
before I went to the laundry, Janie had, in packing
the clean clothes, mixed the tablecloths of two
customers, who, it happened, were near neighbours
and deadly enemies. Janie, finding out her mistake,
went to rectify it, and one of the neighbours, thinking the exchange had been made purposely, took Janie
and shook her until she was at last obliged to drop

the tablecover she had brought and run back to the laundry for dear life.

"Don't you get tired, running about so much from eight in the morning until eight at night?" I asked her one day, when she had just come in from collecting long-overdue accounts.

"No; Hi'm never tired. Hi like to work all the time. Hi don't like Sundays, because Hi 'av' to be quiet."

"Don't you like to read on Sunday?" I asked her.

"Yes, sometimes. Hi always reads the *People* and the *Quiver;* but Hi'd rather work."

I was beginning to get intensely interested in this strange species of laundry-girl, who, as she one day told me, would be "haighteen years hold in Haugust," and was earning "haight" shillings a week. At first I was scarcely able to understand the Cockney dialect over which she was complete mistress; but by degrees I became accustomed to it, and I was really in danger of getting to talk Cockney myself. Several times I discovered her looking curiously at me, and one day she asked me if I had had much "schooling." I answered that I did not know as much as I wished I did; and she began to consider how she might help me.

"When Hi first saw you, Miss Barnes," said she, "Hi said to myself, 'She's a nice young ——'" There Janie stopped, and was lost in meditation. I had half-expected she was going to speak of me as a "young lady;" but no. She appeared to be thinking for a time as to what was the correct word, and then she ended with "person"! However, I had become used to being called a "young person" when I was in service, so I took no offence at Janie's disinclination to place me out of what might be my proper sphere.

On Thursday I was wondering what could have become of the clothes I had sent to the laundry, when Janie unpinned a parcel, and informed me that it had been sent by a new customer, and all the pieces needed marking. They were my own personal property.

"There ought to be some other way of marking clothes, especially the fine ones," I said, as I picked up my best new handkerchief and proceeded to number it. Janie insisted that red cotton could not hurt anything, but I was of a different opinion. It stood to reason that the coarse cotton must soon tear holes in fine linen, but Janie declared that everything must be marked, and she concluded that as it was for a new customer, and she wanted it done nicely, she had better do it herself.

The system of identifying the different articles at the London laundries might certainly be improved. In America the Chinamen have a way of attaching labels by a single thread, which is cut after the clothes have been ironed. This is certainly a much better plan than the use of the disfiguring and ruinous red cotton, although even this trouble might be avoided if all clothes were stamped with the owner's full name before being sent to the laundry.

I one day asked Janie why the place was called a "sanitary laundry." From what I had seen of the Y—— and Z—— Laundry, I could not discover that it was intended to have any very sanitary effects upon the girls that were employed there. Janie thought it was probably sanitary because it was worked by steam, and no chemicals were used. Other laundries used chloride of lime and carbolic acid to whiten the clothes, but the Y—— and Z—— people avoided everything but soda and soap. However, this explanation was hardly satisfactory to me, especially as every morning, and several times during the day, I was obliged to walk through the water from the boilers, and I was getting a sore throat in consequence. It seemed to me there should have been some outlet for the steam, which was sometimes nearly suffocating, and must surely affect the health of the girls, though when I complained of it they assured me I would get used to it in time, and would not notice it. The one room served not only for a laundry, but a small portion of it was used for stabling purposes for the two horses that hauled the delivery waggons. Amid the din of the machinery and the whizzing of the steam, the sound of their pawing and neighing could be heard. When they were taken to and from the waggon, they walked directly through the laundry door, and indeed their so-called stable was only partitioned off on one side, and they were in plain sight all the time. The poor animals must have suffered intensely from the steam and heat of the place. And all this in a "sanitary laundry"!

I will admit that I did not hear any of the girls complain of the inconveniences I have mentioned. They probably saw nothing incongruous in a laundry and stable combined in one! But I am sure that, had the poor beasts been able to talk, they would have had some objections to offer.

When Thursday afternoon came, I began to grow tired of marking and sorting, and I begged Mrs. Morris to let me show my skill in ironing. It was difficult to convince her that I had any talents in that direction. She thought I had better keep to the sorting for several weeks before I attempted ironing. "You must not expect to learn everything in a week. It takes months to learn anything about the laundry trade," she said to me, after I had requested a change of occupation. I told my troubles to Janie, and she, too, laughed at the idea of my leaving off sorting when I had not worked three days. I think I must have looked particularly downhearted at this, for Janie suddenly changed her mind, and said—

"Never mind, Miss Barnes; Hi'll hask Mis' Morris about it in the morning."

CHAPTER III.

A CONTEST WITH FLAT-IRONS.

ON Friday morning I was sent to the "preparing-table" to sprinkle and fold some servants' print dresses. From a distance the work had looked easy enough, but Agnes, the head preparer, who, by the way, bore a striking resemblance to the pictures of the Grand Duchess of Hesse, taught me that there was a special method of distributing the water, and a particular twist and turn to give the sleeves and bodice, to say nothing of the compactness and firmness with which they must be folded up. I was impressed with the kind treatment I received from these girls, who looked upon me as a beginner from their own ranks. Not one but tried to help me over the hard places of my first week's experience, and, despite the awkwardness that I must have displayed in everything I attempted, they tried to encourage me, assuring me that I would get used to things in time.

While Agnes was telling me how hard it had been at first for her to learn the art of shirt-starching, I noticed that an animated conversation was being carried on in another part of the room between Mrs. Morris and Janie. Then Mrs. Morris came over to me, and said she had decided to let me iron a little, and perhaps I would succeed better with it than I had done with marking.

So an extra table was brought into the laundry and fitted up with ironing tools, and, as Mrs. Morris handed me a bag of handkerchiefs, she said—

" Now, mind you don't pay attention to Mrs. Bruckerstone, that stout woman that's beside you. She's the biggest gossip in the place, and will ask you no end of questions about yourself, and tell you all she knows about the other girls."

Then I was seized with an inclination to cultivate Mrs. Bruckerstone's acquaintance.

Mrs. Morris led me to the stove, took up an iron and held it with one hand close to her face.

" That's the way to tell if it's hot enough," she explained.

" But suppose the iron should slip and hit me in the face?" I asked, horrified already at the dangers that loomed in my path.

" You must take your chances about that. How else would you know the iron was right?" she answered.

"Why, try it with my fingers, like this. I always did it so at home;" and then I illustrated the way I had managed with the family ironing in Australia.

"Well, that's not right; but you can do it that way, if you like," was her reply, as she went back to her own table, where she was always surrounded with books and bills.

I thought then that Mrs. Morris had concluded that a girl so afraid of burning her face would hardly do for laundry work, and I had not a doubt but she would tell me so later on; but I went to the table assigned me, and commenced on the handkerchiefs without any regrets. When I had finished my first piece, I thought it time to open conversation with Mrs. Bruckerstone, who stood near me, ironing children's frocks.

"I think you iron beautifully," I remarked, as she returned from the clothes-horse, where she had hung an embroidered baby-dress, which really did her great credit. I could see that I had put myself in Mrs. Bruckerstone's good graces at once, as she replied—

"When ye've been at it long as me, Hi 'ope ye'll hiron as well. Hi've been in the business twenty years."

I observed that, if I ever learned to iron half as well as she did, I'd be content, and then we were friends.

I had supposed I knew how to iron handkerchiefs, but Mrs. Bruckerstone said I needed some instructions, and, though I did very well for a beginner, my method was not quite correct. They must be ironed from hem to hem, and folded together with the red

M

cotton mark on the outside, so that the packer would know to whom they belonged.

"Where ye from?" she asked.

"Near Oxford Circus."

"That's a long waiys off. Must cost ye a pretty penny for trine fare. Ye ought to find lodgings hereabouts."

"Yes, I'm thinking of doing that if I get on all right. I'm only here on trial now."

"Going to be a shirt-hironer or finery-hironer?"

"I want to learn the whole business."

"Then, Hi suppose, yer idee is to be a managress," said Mrs. Bruckerstone, with the accent on the last syllable.

At that time Mrs. Morris was not in hearing, and all the girls began to tell how they expected to spend the coming Bank Holiday, which was Whit Monday. When several had declared their intentions of going to fairs and "theayters," Mrs. Bruckerstone turned to me, and asked how I should celebrate the day. I replied that I thought I should go to Hyde Park.

"Got a young man?" was her next question.

"Oh, yes," I answered.

"What do he do for a living?"

I was about to say I did not know, when I thought it would hardly do to have a young man and confess to ignorance of his occupation, so I said—

"He's a soldier."

"That's nice," said Mrs. Bruckerstone, approvingly. "Agnes's young man's a soldier, too. What's the naime of yours?"

I was getting into deep waters, and I began to flounder, but I wanted to hold on a little longer, so I said—

" His name is Jones."

I thought that would be a perfectly harmless name, but it transpired it was the very one I should have avoided, for my co-worker said—

" Why's that's the naime of Agnes's young man. Hi wonder if they could be the saime! What's his first naime ?"

The waters were getting deeper and deeper. I dared not invent a first name, lest I should chance to hit upon the one that belonged to Agnes's young man. I pictured to myself how, in such an event, that young woman might be transformed from my interested friend into a bitter foe. Then the thought of Australia again saved me.

" They couldn't be the same," I said to Mrs. Bruckerstone; " my Mr. Jones is a soldier in Australia, and I haven't seen him for a year. I didn't say I was going to the park with him."

That set matters right, and I was thankful to have escaped so easily.

" Ye won't make much money at the rate yer hironing," remarked my companion, when, after having stood at the table three hours, I counted my handkerchiefs, and found I had ironed just thirty-four. I was so tired, I could hardly stand. I had several times burned my fingers, and once nearly fallen against the stove. Handkerchiefs were paid for at the rate of a penny a dozen, so, had I been a paid worker, I would have earned less than a penny an hour.

The bag of handkerchiefs was empty, and I felt I must rest from my labours. It wanted fifteen minutes till dinner-time, and I wondered how I

M 2

"LIZZIE BARNES," LAUNDRY-GIRL.

(From a Photograph by the London Stereoscopic Company.)

should ever walk to the queer little restaurant where I bought my midday meal.

"Suppose ye hiron this pinafore for me," said Mrs. Bruckerstone, taking from a hamper a much-embroidered garment, and laying it on my table. "Hiron the needlework on the wrong side, and don't crease it in the middle."

"I'll do it after dinner. I'm so tired, I must rest," I protested; but, looking up, I saw Mrs. Morris's eyes upon me, and, in order to avoid further conversation with the woman, I concluded I had better do the pinafore.

When at the end of twenty minutes I passed it to my teacher for inspection, she seemed surprised that I had done it so well, and announced her conviction that I would make a "finery-hironer," though I was rather slow.

"Ye can 'elp me again this afternoon," she said, as she pinned on her bonnet preparatory to going home for dinner.

All that afternoon I regretted having shown so much skill in the way of pinafore-ironing, for Mrs. Morris told me I might go on and help Mrs. Bruckerstone, only not to talk with her.

After the dinner-hour, another pinafore was handed to me. My burnt fingers were smarting, and my feet were aching from walking to and from the stove. It took me an hour to finish that piece of work, and Mrs. Bruckerstone said it was not done so well as the first. Still, she was not discouraged. Two more pinafores were given me, and had it not been for the fact that I knew she was paid by the day, and not by the piece, I would have suspected she was trying to make money out of me. Finery-ironing was paid for at the rate of three shillings a day. It was done as day work for the reason that some articles were more elaborate than others, and so no average time for doing them up could be calculated upon. In such cases, to pay a stipulated sum for each piece would have been unfair to both employer and employée. Shirt-ironers, I had been told, often added to their own earnings by the work turned out by learners, who, desirous of becoming proficient in the art of polishing, often "gave time" to the extent of several weeks, and sometimes two or three months. What presentable work they did was counted with that of their instructor, who in this way often made a shilling a day extra money. For this reason "piece-workers" were always ready to take pupils.

But I knew Mrs. Bruckerstone could have no such deeply-laid scheme in regard to myself, and I had no doubt that she gave me pinafores to iron because of a genuine desire to help me, although I did not fully appreciate her interest in me. When, at four o'clock, I was still struggling over the third piece, having in the meantime several times sat down on an upturned hamper in order to rest, she began to lose her patience, which heretofore had indeed been Joblike both in quantity and quality.

"Hi see yer not strong enough for a finery-hironer," said she, as for the fifth or sixth time I returned to my position on the hamper. "Hare ye good at figgers?"

I confessed to ignorance of mathematics, and poor Mrs. Bruckerstone looked disheartened, as she replied:

" Hi were going to saiy ye might better work at books in a shop or factory."

Then pointing to some nurses' sleeves which one of the women was ironing, she continued—

" That's the kind of place ye want. Be a 'ospital nurse. Ye looks fit for that, kinder quiet and genteel."

" Hospital patients are too cross and fidgety. I wouldn't like to be a nurse."

Then she grew angry, and declared it was not what I liked, but what I must do. I was a failure at laundry work, and, if I hadn't "schooling" enough to figure, nothing was left for me but the hospital.

At that I stopped resting, and changed my iron preparatory to going on with the pinafore. At tea-time it was finished, and Mrs. Bruckerstone exhibited her lively interest in my welfare by informing the girls that I had been two hours ironing an apron, working five minutes and resting ten throughout the performance; in the face of which she asked their opinion as to whether or not I was likely to succeed in the profession I had chosen. They all agreed that laundry work was not my *forte*, and they put their heads together to think of some other calling which lay more in the line of my peculiar abilities for resting.

One girl suggested that I go into a coffee-house, when Janie's sister interposed that such a situation would be too rough. Someone else asked me how I would like to be a barmaid ; but, when Mrs. Bruckerstone gave the information that barmaids had often to keep books as well as pour out drinks, that idea was given up. Dressmaking was spoken of, but

Miss Stebbins, who had seen some of my early efforts at marking, and did not know of my lately-attained skill through Janie's instructions, expressed it as her opinion that I was not likely to succeed in any department of needlework. Attendance in a baker's shop next came up for discussion, and then Janie, who all this time had been keeping up a quiet thinking, announced that she thought a place in a nice confectioner's in the West-End would be just the thing for me. All the girls coincided with her in this, and so they settled it among themselves that I was to dispense cream chocolates and peppermint drops from behind a counter.

So great had been the anxiety exhibited in regard to my future, and so earnest did the girls seem in advising me how to gain a livelihood, that, before tea-time was over, even I had become terrified at the outlook, and had worked myself up into the " alone-in-London " state of feeling. For the moment I had a vague apprehension of impending misfortunes, but Mr. Morris's shrill call of " Half-past five ! " which sent every girl to her work, brought me back to my senses, and, telling the girls that I thought I would try the confectioner's shop, I accompanied Mrs. Bruckerstone to the ironing-table, and proceeded to iron the fourth and last garment. Then Mrs. Morris sent Janie with some towels and stockings, with the message that, when I had ironed them, I might come to her, as she had other work that she wished me to do.

Towels and stockings completed, I was again almost overcome with " that tired feeling," and I went to Mrs. Morris with the hope that there might be no incompatibility between a chair and the work she had picked out for me.

She and Janie were examining a large counterpane which had been torn in the wash by too energetic boiling. "Suppose we red cotton hit, Mis' Morris?" said Janie; "that will maike them think hit was done before hit caime here." By that time I had learned that to "red cotton" anything meant to put a few large stitches in an article that had been torn before its arrival at the laundry, and I thought Janie's idea of disposing of the torn counterpane a very brilliant one.

"Here, Miss Barnes, you can sit down and darn up all these holes," said Mrs. Morris, handing the counterpane to me. Wishing I were back at the ironing-board, I took the quilt and sat down to needlework and despair. At first, like the bad work-woman that I was, I complained of my tools. The cotton was too coarse for the needle, and the thimble loaned me was far too large. I declared I could not sew under such conditions, and when Janie, out of the kindness of her heart, removed them, by lending me a large needle and a small thimble, my troubles were only increased. When done, the last state of the counterpane was no improvement on the first; and when I handed it to Janie she looked first at my handiwork, then at me, and, with a pitifully resigned expression on her face, said—

"You'll 'ave to taike it hout, Miss Barnes, and Hi'll do it when Mis' Morris goes into the 'ouse."

It was then that my affection for Janie reached its highest point, and I determined that her kindness to me should not go unrewarded.

" How long did you go to school, Janie ? " I asked.

" Hi went through the seventh standard, Miss Barnes ; then Hi 'ad to work. How far did you go in books ? "

" Oh, a little farther than that," I answered evasively.

" Hit's too bad you can't teach in a Board School, Miss Barnes. Do you think you'll get a plaice at a confectioner's ? You might do that work, but som'ow I can't 'elp worrying. Hit seems so 'ard for you to learn things ! "

Janie went on with her packing with a far-away look in her eyes, as though she were trying to think up some way by which I might be made capable of earning a livelihood. I also fell into a reverie concerning Janie. Unlike myself, it did not seem hard for her to " learn things," and I pictured her nervous little fingers flying over the keys of the typewriter, while I dictated to her the results of my future journalistic investigations.

CHAPTER IV.

THE DAY OF MY RESIGNATION.

SATURDAY morning was the busiest time of all the week. The ironing was to be finished, and the clothes folded, packed in hampers, and delivered. It was a day of little rest for the horses, but they probably enjoyed the pulling and hauling in the fresh air much better than breathing the steam-laden atmosphere of their so-called " stable."

The skill displayed by Miss Stebbins and Janie in

.elling at a moment's inquiry just which numbers were meant for each of the customers was a source of wonder to me. The Y—— and Z—— Laundry had a good "trade," not only in the various parts of London, but in several of the surrounding suburbs. Between four and five hundred regular customers were enrolled on the books, so that the numbers which marked the clothes ranged all the way from one upwards. To be able to know five hundred people by number as well as by name seemed as marvellous a matter to me as the much-discussed dexterity of the head waiters in Chicago hotels, who can hand out the hat that belongs to each of two or three hundred men, and never make a mistake, though the hats are all alike.

When one of the loads was nearly ready for delivery, I heard rather an interesting discussion between Mrs. Morris and John, the driver. I learned that the securing of credit with his laundryman depended much upon the neighbourhood in which a man lived, the number of servants he kept, and, above all, the quantity and the quality of the shirts he sent to the wash. The customer who soiled fourteen shirts in a week was trusted implicitly, while he who sent only seven or less, with the brand of a less fashionable furnishing house upon them, was not given so long a time. Then there was the customer who wore coloured shirts during the week and white ones on Sundays and Bank Holidays, who must needs pay for his goods on delivery. Some of the accounts were allowed to run from three months to a year, others were required to be settled monthly, and with still others the rule was "pay down."

"Shall I leave this 'amper, ma'am, if they doesn't pay?" asked John of Mrs. Morris, as he shouldered a large basket and started for the waggon.

"Well, it's a new customer," said Mrs. Morris; "but they live in a good street, and all the clothes are of the finest quality. Yes, just leave them, and ask if they want a laundry-book."

"But they rents their 'ouse furnished, ma'am; the 'ousemaid told me so," persisted John.

"Oh, that's different! Better collect the money, then. There's no knowing how long they'll stop there!" answered Mrs. Morris.

It seemed that the people who rented furnished houses were allowed no quarter at the Y—— and Z—— Laundry.

I also discovered that the keepers of laundries knew quite as much about the private affairs of their customers as do the butcher and baker and other tradespeople. John had many a tale to tell of certain strange things that housemaid, cook, and butler related to him concerning the home-life of master and mistress. The kitchen-door confidences that passed between him and the servants, when he made his weekly "rounds," sometimes made entertaining gossip for the laundry-girls. When I heard some of this interesting talk, it occurred to me that it might be as well if all areas were fitted up with some sort of patent lifts, by which transactions with tradesmen could be carried on at a distance. It would certainly save much time, and family affairs might then be kept more closely at home.

But, so far as Mrs. Morris was concerned, the only personal interest she took in her customers was in regard to the question of their ability to pay their accounts. She was one of the most clever and indefatigable business women I had ever seen. No one in the laundry worked as hard or as many hours in the day as herself. She inspected every department, and there was not a branch of the business with which she was not familiar. She had piercing black eyes, that showed her capabilities in the way of bargain-getting, and her nose was of the kind that physiognomists say denotes acquisitiveness. She was short and wiry, and, though under thirty years of age, she was more round-shouldered than many women of sixty. However, in this respect she resembled her employées, for there was not a straight-backed girl among them, and in some instances their shoulders were so bent that it amounted almost to a deformity. A few of the women were positively humped, and they made an uncanny sight as they stood over the ironing-boards. I spoke of it one day to Janie, and she replied, "Yes, Miss Barnes, all laundry-girls gets that waiy;" and I have since observed that stooping shoulders are a peculiarity among them.

Mr. Morris, with the assistance of a small boy, attended to the management of the engine and the machinery, while his wife overlooked everything else. She was even able to take his place if he was absent for a day. Both, though of somewhat better education than those who served them, had evidently sprung from the ranks of the lower classes, and their ambition to get on in the world was boundless. Believing in the proverb, "If you want anything done, do it yourself," they worked early and late, scarcely taking time to eat. Every morning, at seven o'clock,

Mrs. Morris was in the laundry to see that all was in readiness for the girls to commence at eight. She breakfasted at half-past seven, and fifteen minutes later she was again at her post, where she remained until dinner-time. She ate dinner in twenty minutes, and was back before any of the girls had returned. At night, when the laundry was closed, she took her books to the house, and it was sometimes as late as one or two o'clock in the morning when she had them settled. On one occasion, during the week I was there, she told me she had run thirty pairs of curtains through the ironing-machine after ten o'clock at night. She was not in any way unkind or unjust with the women she employed, rather putting herself on an equality with them, and demanding no work from them that she was not able and willing to perform herself. If any heavy lifting was to be done, she was always foremost in the fray.

On Saturday, I noticed that she examined every piece of clothes before it was returned to the customers, and, if any article was badly gotten up, it was washed and ironed over again, even though she was obliged to do it herself. She was scrupulously conscientious as to the manner in which the most unimportant part of the work was performed, and she would not, under any consideration, allow injurious chemicals to be used in the washing, no matter how much they might lighten the labour or lessen time. She carefully measured the amount of soda that was put into the washers, and the soap used was of the best quality. Any articles from which the colour had been taken out in the washing or boiling were laid aside for her special attention, and she restored lost blues, pinks, and other colours by dipping them into a solution of acetic acid. If, through careless handling in the laundry, spots of iron-rust got on the linen, she immediately applied salts of lemon to remove them. When goods already iron-rusted were brought to her, she charged a penny for each treatment.

However, there was one thing she allowed that rather surprised me : that was the stringing of several collars and cuffs together before putting them in the washer. It was a good plan for keeping each person's collars separated from the others, but it had a tendency to tear out the button-holes.

The girls at the Y—— and Z——· Laundry, unlike those employed in most places, were allowed to have their own work done at a slightly cheaper rate than that of the ordinary customers. Saturday afternoon I watched Janie hand to the women the small parcels containing their own personal property, and I wondered how girls earning from three to twenty shillings a week could be willing to pay out four or five pence for the doing up of a white skirt or ruffled blouse. Some of their bills amounted to over a shilling.

Mrs. Bruckerstone had taken to the laundry, early in the week, a baby's bonnet, which was supposed to belong to someone in her family, so that the usual reduction was made in the price of it. Over the ironing of that bonnet there had been a near approach to a fight. The bonnet, with several others, was given to one of the women to iron, and when it was finished and hung on the horse the appearance did not please Mrs. Bruckerstone, so she got out her own bonnet-board and re-ironed it, saying it belonged to a neighbour of hers, and therefore must be done up extra well. The woman who had at first ironed it took the insult so much to heart that she turned informer, and reported to Mrs. Morris that Mrs. Bruckerstone had given out that she was the only proper "bunnit-hironer" in the place, and that, moreover, Mrs. Bruckerstone had been attempting to get reduced rates for her neighbours by passing off their goods as her own.

Then Mrs. Morris announced that all neighbours must be charged full price, and Mrs. Bruckerstone's face wore a crestfallen look, when, as she was paying her bill, an additional penny was charged for the unlucky bonnet.

At a little after two o'clock there was a lull in the motions of the machinery, which showed that no more washing would be done that week. Each ironer continued to work until her particular lot of things was finished, and at about half-past three, all the girls were paid off for the week. The lowest wages were those earned by the smaller girls of about fifteen or sixteen years of age, who attended to the smoothing of towels and table-linen by putting them in and pulling them out of the large ironing-machine. Their portion was from three to six shillings a week. Agnes, the preparer, received eleven shillings ; Annie Martin, who stood at the collar-machine, was paid fourteen shillings ; Mrs. Bruckerstone had three shillings a day for the time she had worked, which amounted to about five days ; Janie's sister and her companions in shirt-ironing drew from fifteen to twenty-three shillings, according to their talents ; the girl who presided over the washtub received twelve shillings, and Miss Stebbins had fifteen shillings. Miss Stebbins was the only girl among them who did not live "home." She resided in apartments near the laundry, and for board and lodging paid out ten of the fifteen shillings. Saturday nights she went to the country to stop until Monday, the train fare costing her another shilling, so she had four shillings left over for clothes and extras. When paid off, all the women, except Janie and Miss Stebbins, left the laundry to remain away until the following Tuesday, and as they went out of the door they were talking of various plans for Bank Holiday.

The regular hours were from eight until eight, with twenty minutes for eleven-o'clock luncheon, an hour for dinner, and half an hour for tea. I had several times heard the girls discussing the proposed amendment to the Factory Act ; but among them the idea seemed to prevail that the new law was to be an eight-hour law, which would reduce their hours of labour from eight in the morning until six at night. Those women who received their wages by the day or the week were in favour of having the hours reduced, while those who did piecework preferred to put in their time as they wished. This feeling was, of course, quite natural, for the ironers did not usually commence work until late Monday afternoon, and finished the week at a little after two on Saturday, thus making only five full days in the week. However, the regular hours at the Y—— and Z—— Laundry were about what the Factory Act demands, so that Mrs. Morris knew she had no cause to trouble

N

herself about that phase of the matter. Quite often many of the girls were obliged to work overtime until nine or ten at night, but I was told that in such cases the overtime was not paid for—most of the employées receiving a weekly wage, and it was expected that they would remain in the place until the work required of them was finished. So far as I could discover, few of them had any complaints to make in regard to the hours. Some of them had been employed in laundries where the hours were much longer, Annie Martin having recently left a situation where the regular hours were from eight in the morning until eleven at night.

Janie and Miss Stebbins were the two most often called upon to stop late, and were always the last to leave. While the other girls had a part, if not all, of the Saturday half-holiday, they were expected to stop with Mrs. Morris until the last parcel of goods was placed in the delivery waggon. On the Saturday preceding Bank Holiday it was after seven o'clock when the two girls quitted their posts, but both of them attended to their duties cheerfully, and took it all as a matter of course Janie, according to her own statement, was not tired, only a little "muddled," and she regretted that such a thing as a Bank Holiday should exist, preferring rather to go to her work the next Monday as usual.

On the whole, the girls were a fairly contented set, although the inconveniences under which they did their work was a trial to those who had held situations in more comfortably arranged places. Nearly all of them objected to the cement floor, which, they said, made their feet ache. It certainly would have entailed but little expense on the part of the proprietor to have had at least a portion of the room boarded over ; and the ironers, who were constantly obliged to walk to and from the stove, would have greatly appreciated a wooden floor. Some of the machinery, too, needed fencing in to make it less dangerous to those who were continually passing so very close to it as to make it highly probable that their skirts would be caught when the wheels were in motion. During my first two days I several times very narrowly escaped coming in collision with the hydro-extractor. There should also have been an arrangement for carrying off the steam, the odour from which was most sickening, and the need of an air-propeller, or fanning-machine, was very apparent. The constantly wet floor was another thing that must have been prejudicial to the health of those in the place.

Indeed, taken as a whole, the sanitary conditions of the laundry could hardly have been worse ; and, if the proposed amendment is passed, some of its restrictive clauses will readily apply to the state of things at the Y—— and Z—— Laundry. It is no excuse for Mr. and Mrs. Morris to say that they have only lately gone into business, and cannot be expected to have all the comforts and conveniences of long-established laundries. Decency, as well as the laws of health, would demand that a few pounds be expended in fitting up the place to make it properly habitable for themselves, their workpeople, and their horses. The one large room in which the work is now done should be divided into at least three apartments wash-house, sorting-room, and ironing-room.

When I engaged at the laundry, I had expected

N 2

to spend between eight and ten days there ; but Saturday brought me such a weariness of the flesh that I decided I had better resign my situation before Mrs. Morris should have time to inform me that she did not consider me up to the mark for a laundry-worker.

" I'm afraid I'm not strong enough for this sort of thing, Mrs. Morris," I said, as, standing with Janie in the doorway, I bade her good-night.

" I was going to speak of that myself," she replied. " Somehow, you don't seem to have very much energy, and I would advise you to go into an easier kind of business."

Energy ! If she had only known the large amount of that article it had required to keep me in her laundry for five days, I am sure she would have changed her mind.

" Miss Barnes is going to a confectioner's, Mis' Morris," said Janie, in a sort of defensive way, as though she thought I needed a champion.

So my brief and very chequered career as a laundry-girl ended ; but, not having yet gained as much knowledge of the work and the workers as I wished, I determined to spend the following week among the laundry-girls in different parts of London, to discover if, after all, they were such a formidable and badly-treated class of individuals.

CHAPTER V.

"SOAP-SUDS ISLAND" AND THE EAST-END.

ACTON is a village of tubs and clothes-lines. So many of its inhabitants are engaged in laundry-work, in a large and small way, that the place has been given the name of "Soap-suds Island."

On Tuesday afternoon I went to Acton to make the acquaintance of the girls, whom I had heard from many quarters were typical representatives of their class.

I waited for some time outside the gates of one of the large laundries, where many young girls were employed. At a little after seven o'clock the gates were swung back, and I found myself in a crowd of some forty or fifty women of all sizes and ages. I opened conversation by asking one of them the way to the station, and then I explained that I had come out to visit the laundry and wanted to interview them in regard to their opinion of the application of the Factory Act to laundries. They became interested at once, and, though some of them were woefully ignorant as to just what the Factory Act was, they one and all declared themselves in favour of shorter hours. I learned that at some of the laundries the girls commenced at six o'clock in the morning and worked until between seven and nine at night, according to whether or not it was a busy part of the season. At half-past seven they were allowed a half-hour for breakfast, which most of them carried with them.

A little later I was invited to visit the Working Girls' Club, an organisation of laundry-girls started a few years ago by a number of ladies who became interested in helping them. There I introduced myself properly, told the girls how I had spent a week in a laundry, and that, wanting to know more about those engaged in the work, had come out to Acton. The fact that I had done laundry-work, no matter for what purpose, put me in their good graces at once, and they treated me as one of themselves, inviting me to become a member of the club by the payment of fourpence a month, the fee required of each member. The little room in which they met had been very comfortably fitted up. One corner at the back served for a sort of pantry, where tea was made on a small paraffin stove, and served to the girls by two young ladies who had been appointed to be their entertainers for the evening.

I was told that it was not until some time after the club was started that the girls could be induced to say "Miss" and "Mrs." in addressing the officers, among whom were some of the best-known ladies in Acton. At the time of my visit, however, they had become accustomed to showing a certain amount of respect to their superiors.

"Hi there, miss, I've fetched a copper and wants caike and tea," called out one girl to a quiet young lady who was boiling the kettle in the back of the room.

"Very well, Lucy," she answered smilingly, without a sign of annoyance, and then a cup of tea and box of cake were brought to the table, where about twenty girls were gathered for what they termed "a bite." It was an interesting thing to me to watch this young lady taking the part of a servant and administering to the wants of the laundry-girls, who, despite the amusing familiarity of that "Hi there, miss," tried to the best of their ability to show proper respect by saying, "Thank 'ee, miss," when their orders were carried out. I joined them in their late tea, paying the stipulated price, a halfpenny for cake and the same for a cup of tea, including milk and sugar.

The girls poured their tea into their saucers, and setting the cups on the table, made ugly rings on the red cover.

" See, you soil the table-cloth, putting the cups on it like that," I suggested to the girl who sat next me, drinking her tea from a saucer, while she held the dripping spoon in front of her.

" Yes, miss, I sees it," she answered, and then turning to her companions, called out, " It's a shaime, girls. The laidy says we's spiling the cloth with the tea-cups. We must hold 'em in the other 'and when we drinks out the saucer."

I noticed that most of them were very young, probably under eighteen. Their costumes were of the coster order, but many, if properly dressed, would have been good-looking young women.

After tea, the lady who had served it was requested to " maike some tunes on the pianer," which she did with a right good will. Then the place was turned into a ball-room, and as each girl chose a partner, I was invited to " taike a turn." With first one and then another of the girls I joined them in their schottische to the tune of " Knocked 'em in the Old Kent Road," many of the girls singing as well as dancing. Then followed a polka to " Ta-ra-ra-boom-de-ay," and the programme ended with waltzing " After the ball was over," for which dance I had offered me a choice of a dozen partners.

It was then nearly half-past nine, and, as one of the girls declared " the young laidy couldn't go to the staition alone," I left the club-room with an escort of five girls, who showed the liveliest interest in taking proper care of me. All the way to the station they

kept up a continual talking on various subjects.
They told me that a few of the girls at one of the
laundries had lately joined the Salvation Army, and
that there had been a "grait chainge" in them.
Then they discussed the "Factory Hact," and begged
me to use my influence in their behalf. They were
not in favour of the hours that obliged them to be up
before a little after five every morning and hurry off

"'CARN'T YER SEE WE'VE GOT A YOUNG LAIDY WITH US?'"

to work at six without even so much as a cup of tea
or coffee to stay them until the breakfast-hour.

Once, when we had nearly reached the station, a
crowd of boys in front of a public-house began throw-
ing pebbles. One of my protectors threw back a
missile with the injunction—

"Better behaive there! Carn't yer see we've got a
young laidy with us?" and I could not help thinking

what a pity they could not have a " young laidy " with them oftener. Who could foresee the results that such a state of things might bring about !

As my train moved out from the station, the girls ran along the platform as far as they could, giving me numerous farewell messages, and the last I heard from them was—

" Saiy, miss, don't forget to maike 'em give us that Hact you told about."

Having an invitation to visit their club on Sunday that I might inspect them in what they called their " church togs," I made them another call on that day, and found every girl arrayed in her Sunday best. Cotton velvet was in great requisition, blue the favourite colour, and long plumed hats the ruling things in headgear. In the jewellery line heavy silver chains and lockets and threepenny-bit ear-rings were greatly in demand. Sunday afternoons they were allowed their tea without payment, the cost being covered by the subscription fee of fourpence a month. When I arrived, most of them had just returned from church, and had sundry original remarks to make about the service and the people in attendance.

So I had mixed with the Acton girls, and suffered no bodily injury or moral contamination in consequence ! I did not go with the expectation of finding a great degree of refinement among them, and I was in no way disappointed. It is true that I may have met only the best of them, and I have no doubt that, had I remained long among them, some unpleasant knowledge would have been brought to me ; but, on the whole, considering the circumstances of their bringing up and their early surroundings, I could not see that they were deserving of the opprobrium that I had heard cast upon them.

Some time afterwards, accompanied by a young woman, who was herself a laundress, and had been appointed to make a report of the opinions of laundry employers and workers in regard to the Factory Act, I made a trip among the smaller establishments of the East-End. A few of the employers had not heard of the proposed amendment, and did not understand what it was about ; but on general principles they were opposed to it, and ordered us out of their shops. In Brick Lane, Whitechapel, I visited a laundry that took in the shirts and "starched work" from the inhabitants of the neighbouring streets. Friday was the busy day at this place, for the reason that many of the customers were Jews, who, no matter how they dressed on other days, were always careful to garb themselves in clean white shirts for their Sabbath day. The proprietor of the laundry told me that quite often, when the work had not been finished up Friday night, some of his customers would come into the shop early Saturday morning, and, with their coats buttoned up to their throats, wait about until their shirts were ironed, and then request the privilege of putting them on before going out into the street. This was the sort of place, too, where the young man who owns but one collar and one "front" always has them done up in time for Bank Holiday.

In this laundry, as well as in the several other establishments in the neighbourhood of Whitechapel, I had an opportunity to become acquainted with many of the women employed in the ironing-rooms.

I discovered that most laundry-girls married at a very
early age. In fact, I found but few girls over twenty
who were without husbands. One very pretty young
woman smilingly told me that she had only been
married the day before, and had come immediately
back to her post as collar-dresser. Asking her why
she married, when she saw no prospect of bettering
her condition, she replied that she liked the work,
and would not, if she could, remain at home all day.
All of these young wives had what they called "homes"
—that is, two, three, or four rooms, with their own
furniture in them. The girl who married and continued to live with her parents or in lodgings was
looked down upon as being particularly unfortunate
or improvident. One young woman said that ever
since she commenced work, at twelve years of age,
she had been laying by a small sum each week
against the day of her marriage, in order to purchase dishes, linen, and other things necessary for
the fitting up of a home.

"But how did you know you would get married?"
I asked.

"We all gets married. We has plenty of chances,
never fear," was her answer, and she eyed me suspiciously, as if wondering whether I had meant to
insinuate that she was likely to have no "chances."

To the minds of these girls the idea of marriage
came as a matter of course. One girl confided to me
that she had simply married because the other girls
did. She was not going to have people say that
nobody had ever asked her. That was an imputation that no laundry-girl with any self-respect
could endure.

Yet, notwithstanding the popularity of matrimony, none of them thought for an instant of giving up their trade. They said they returned to the work not so much because they must, as because they liked it. There appeared to be little or no domesticity about them. In the mornings they either left their husbands in charge of the rooms, or they locked the place up until the evening when they returned. Those who had children hired some old person—either a relative or a neighbour—to take care of them, at the rate of about three shillings a head weekly. When four or five children from the same family were to be looked after, there was a small reduction made. These laundry-workers were not without their theories concerning woman's "emancipation." When they married they had no thoughts of giving up what they termed their "independence." They clung to that with the greatest tenacity, and were under the impression that, by earning from ten to twenty shillings a week in a laundry, they were able to hold it fast. In a word, they all seemed "laundry-struck," and marriage seemed to mean no more to them than an escape from being called an "old maid."

In most of the places that I visited the workers considered a certain daily portion of beer necessary to the proper performance of their duties. Some of the employers gave them a daily allowance; others, though refusing to supply it for their employées, permitted them to get it for themselves; while in first-class places, where no beer was allowed on the premises, the women went to the public-houses and drank it at dinner and tea-time. In the ranks of laundresses, teetotalism is looked upon with suspicion and ridicule.

In their opinion, a glass of beer is as essential to the correct ironing of a dozen shirts as is the flat-iron itself. I believe the amount considered necessary on which to do a good day's work (not counting "over-time," which demands a special allowance) is one and a half pints. If something could be done to convince not only laundry-women, but workers in other trades, that these two things, beer and early marriages, are their greatest hindrances in the way of social and intellectual progress an incalculable amount of good would come to all England.

All the women were interested in the Factory Act, although some of them had not heard of its proposed application to laundries until it was explained to them. Some of the daily and weekly workers expressed the opinion that even factory hours were unjust, when it was taken into consideration that the day of certain working men lasted only eight hours. Of course, in the laundries, Monday is not a busy day, the work seldom commencing until the afternoon, so that with the Saturday half-holiday, only five full days could be given; but the majority of the workers preferred working Monday mornings, and being allowed to leave off earlier in the evening, which, they explained, could be easily managed if the employers would be willing to so arrange it.

Most of the pieceworkers favoured the factory hours. It would really appear that regular hours from eight until six would be much better for all concerned. Many people, while deploring the ignorant condition of laundry-girls, do not stop to consider that their long hours give them really no time for self-improvement, even though they desired it. Only geniuses rise above their surroundings and surmount difficulties without other help; and, as geniuses are rare and ordinary people are numerous, it is almost useless to attempt to do anything for laundry-workers under present conditions. If the hours of the young girls, at least, could be reduced so that their day would commence at eight and end at six, then night-schools might be established in the neighbourhoods of the large laundries, and from eight until ten the girls could be instructed and amused. Even though the Factory Act is made to apply to laundries, that requires them to work until eight o'clock. These hours are too long for girls between twelve and sixteen years of age, and it would seem that some special provision should be made for them.

Many of the mothers, to their disgrace be it said, are opposed to any shorter hours for their daughters on the ground that it will give them more time to get into mischief! I had this reply from several women whose daughters were employed in laundries where the hours were from six in the morning until seven or eight at night. And these women, twenty years ago, married " because the other girls married," and then left their children to be taken care of for three shillings a week! At twelve the girls were put to laundry-work, and henceforth left to their own devices. There is not much wonder that they got into " mischief," and no one is so much to blame for it as their own mothers. To ignorance, more than to a natural inclination for vice, may be ascribed all the immorality that is said to exist among laundry-girls. That there should be immorality under such conditions is no more cause for surprise than that the whitest snow should become tinged with the black of the smoke through which it falls.

So far as I have become acquainted with laundry-girls, I would say that they are not so bad a set as is commonly supposed. They are kind-hearted, and would go out of their way to help the more unfortunate of their own class. They are grateful to anyone who really tries to help them in the right way, which is by putting oneself as much as possible on a level with them and not attempting to show any superiority. To the person who " puts on airs " these girls have a peculiar method of showing their disapproval, whether she be a worker in the laundry or a benevolent lady from the West-End.

I have discovered that injurious chemicals are not nearly so much used in first-class places as many agitators would lead us to believe. Carbolic acid and chloride of lime are more often made use of in the smaller hand laundries than in the steam laundries, although in the latter places the large quantities of soda and cheap soaps might be considerably lessened.

I spent one day in searching for the " laundry dens," of which I had read and heard so much. I found a few places where the sign, " Washing and Mangling," led me up or down some dozens of rickety stairs to rooms where I was informed that " a laidy took in washing ; " but the clothes washed belonged to people but little above the washerwoman herself in station. On inquiring the names of their customers, I was given certain addresses where mostly working men of the lower orders lived. Such " laundries " are not patronised by first-class people, although the sweating system, which is followed by some superior laundries, may sometimes bring about serious results to their customers. These places, which are really the most dangerous in London, sublet the work they receive to women living in miserable hovels, and then pass it off on their customers as having been done in their own establishments.

From the large steam laundries there is nothing to fear in this direction. It is only the smaller laundries that countenance the sweating system. However, it would doubtless be a good plan if all would personally inspect the places where they send their clothes, and demand references from those who apply for their custom. Such a course would, perhaps, save them all the wear and tear of nerves that I experienced when I started out in quest of " Mrs. Johnstone," who lived " somewhere near 'Ammersmith."

THE END.

CPSIA information can be obtained at www.ICGtesting.com
Printed in the USA
BVOW061805200912

300910BV00005BA/7/P

9 781172 245802